LANDSCAPE
PYROGRAPHY
TECHNIQUES & PROJECTS

A Beginner's Guide to Burning by Layer for Beautiful Results

LORA S. IRISH

FOX CHAPEL
PUBLISHING

ACKNOWLEDGMENTS

I wish to extend my deepest thanks to Chris Reggio, Colleen Dorsey, and Wendy Reynolds for their excellent work in the creation, development, and refinement of this manuscript. As an author, it is a wonderful experience to be working with such a well-skilled team.

© 2018 by Lora S. Irish and Fox Chapel Publishing Company, Inc., 903 Square Street, Mount Joy, PA 17552.

Landscape Pyrography Techniques & Projects is an original work, first published in 2018 by Fox Chapel Publishing Company, Inc. The patterns contained herein are copyrighted by the author. Readers may make copies of these patterns for personal use. The patterns themselves, however, are not to be duplicated for resale or distribution under any circumstances. Any such copying is a violation of copyright law.

ISBN 978-1-56523-931-9

The Cataloging-in-Publication Data is on file with the Library of Congress.

To learn more about the other great books from Fox Chapel Publishing, or to find a retailer near you, call toll-free 800-457-9112 or visit us at *www.FoxChapelPublishing.com*.

We are always looking for talented authors. To submit an idea, please send a brief inquiry to acquisitions@foxchapelpublishing.com.

Printed in Singapore
First printing

INTRODUCTION

Pyrography is the art of creating simple line designs, highly detailed renderings, and finely shaded and shadowed drawings using a hot-tipped pen. As the electrically heated pen is pulled across the surface of the chosen medium, the tip literally burns the medium to create varying tonal value lines. The most common and familiar medium used in pyrography is wood, which is where the oft-used term "woodburning" comes from, although pyrography is done on many other media as well, such as paper, leather, and gourds.

The pattern of lines and shading strokes that you use in your pyrography work determines the art style of the finished piece. Any pattern can be worked in any art style or in a combination of styles. In this book, you will encounter many different styles of burning and be able to try small practice patterns for each style so you can discover which styles you prefer. You'll learn about pen tips, temperature settings, fill patterns, and everything else you need to know to set yourself up for success.

Everything you learn will enable you to burn interesting, textured, lifelike landscapes with your pyrography tools and chosen media. You'll be amazed at the variety and realism of what you can create. So without further ado, dive in and start burning!

CONTENTS

15

176

10

26

66

38

127

167

1

Basic Supplies and Techniques

A pyrography project is created using four basic elements: the burning unit, the pen tips, the medium on which you are working, and the pattern or design you will burn. There is also a host of important basic techniques, finishes, and tricks that you'll want to know to maximize your skills and ensure your finished piece turns out just how you want it. We'll cover pen tips in detail in a later chapter, but for now, it's time to learn about all the basic supplies and techniques, starting with burning units.

Burning Units

There are three styles of burning units: one-temperature tools, rheostat-controlled tools, and variable-temperature tools. Which one you choose depends on both the depth of your interest in the craft and your budget.

ONE-TEMPERATURE UNITS

One-temperature burning units are very similar to soldering irons. The solid interchangeable tips are made from brass and screw into the front end of the burning unit. When this tool is plugged into the wall outlet, it heats to a single temperature: high. The most commonly used solid brass tip is called a universal tip. This is the tip shown on the burning unit below, and can be used for both fine line work and shading work. The other common solid tips that are available for this type of burning unit are the calligraphy tip, used for lettering, and the flow tip, used for large area shading.

A full range of tonal values can be burned using a one-temperature tool. Burn pale tones as the tool tip begins to heat; save the darkest tones for when the tool tip has reached its full heat capacity.

RHEOSTAT TOOLS

A rheostat burning unit has a rheostat on the power cord that allows you to fully control the temperature of the pen tip. A rheostat burning unit uses the same interchangeable brass tips as a one-temperature tool. The tonal values that you can see in the practice board below are worked by controlling the pressure of the tip on the wood, the speed of the stroke, and the density of the lines burned, and by adjusting the rheostat temperature setting.

The color tones that you burn using this type of burning unit are controlled by the texture pattern and speed at which you burn. Moving the tool slowly will create a black/brown line. If you speed up your movement, the line color will become paler.

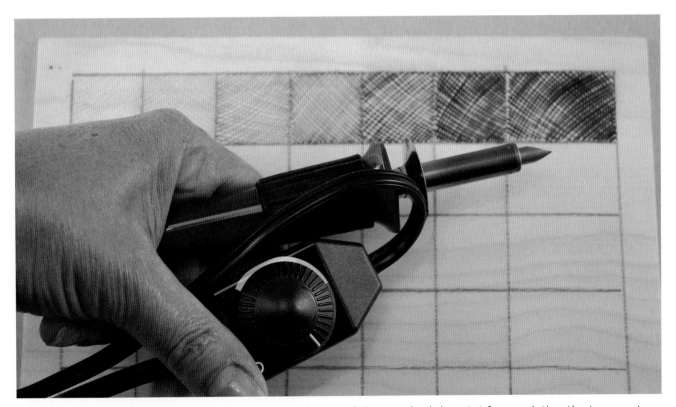

Here you can see an inexpensive beginner's pen, along with its attached rheostat for regulating the temperature.

VARIABLE-TEMPERATURE UNITS

Variable-temperature units have a thermostat base that can be set in a wide temperature range, from very cool at setting number 1 to extremely hot at setting number 10. Because this type of unit has such a wide range of temperatures, you will need to discover which settings are best for your projects. You can accurately set the tip temperature to easily reproduce consistent tonal values in your work. This high level of control ensures that the pen tip remains at a constant temperature as you work.

I use both the Colwood Detailer unit and the Optima 1 Dual unit on a regular basis, and highly recommend either unit as your mainstay burning unit. Both systems provide a wide, reliable temperature range. I tend to use only a small portion of their potential power, setting my temperature settings at 2-3 for pale tones, 3-4 for medium tones, and 5-6 for the darkest tones.

The **Optima 1 Dual unit** has a dual-pen system that allows you to have two burning tips ready for work at all times. A simple toggle switch lets you move from one pen to the next quickly. The pens for this unit have foam grips, which dramatically reduce the heat you feel during a long burning session. The temperature range of the thermostat is excellent and will give you total control over your tonal values.

The **Colwood Detailer unit**, with its single pen, has a wide range of temperature settings. Changing fixed-tip pens or changing tips on the interchangeable-tip pens is quick and easy. The temperature dial system responds quickly for fast tonal value changes. This particular unit can reach very hot temperatures; creating extreme black tones is simply a matter of turning up the heat. The cork handles are very comfortable and dramatically reduce the heat transfer from the tip to your hand.

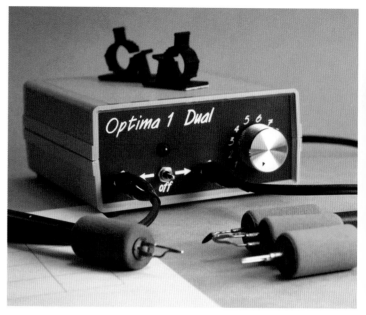

Optima 1 Dual burning unit

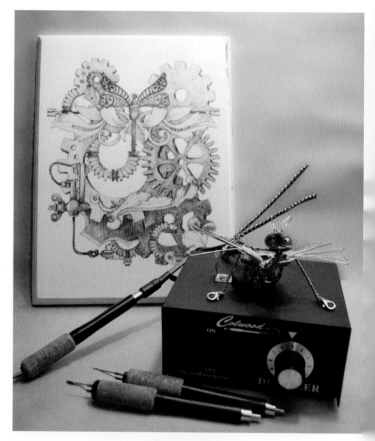

Colwood Detailer burning unit

Cleaning Your Pen Tips

The best-burned strokes are made with a clean, bright tip. As you burn, the tips of your pens will begin to collect residue from the wood sap and carbon buildup from the burned wood. The tips can become so coated with carbon that they take on a black, crusted finish. That black carbon can even be transferred to your project and will appear as long, thin, dark gray streaks in the work. It also can cause your tip to lose heat or create uneven distribution of the heat to your tip.

I use two methods for cleaning my pen tips: emery cloth, and a woodcarving strop with aluminum or red oxide rouging compound. I also clean my tips frequently, long before the carbon buildup can become too intense. Before beginning to clean a pen tip, always unplug the burning unit and allow the pen to fully cool. A hot pen tip can burn both emery cloth and leather strops.

600-grit or finer emery cloth, which can be purchased at your local hardware store, can be used to clean badly encrusted tips. Fold the emery cloth to a size small enough to secure it with your fingers. Gently pull the tip of the pen over the cloth. Use as little pressure as possible as you clean the tip, to avoid distorting or bending the tip.

A leather or synthetic woodcarving strop, used to sharpen woodcarving tools, makes a wonderful cleaning board for any pen tip. Prepare the strop with a coating of either aluminum oxide powder or any fine-grit rouging compound. Pull the tip across the strop, using gentle pressure, until the tip is clean and bright.

After cleaning your pen tip using one of these methods, wipe it and the pen shaft with a clean, dry cloth to remove any remaining carbon particles.

Cleaning the carbon buildup from your pen tips allows you to create clean, crisp burned lines.

Burning Surfaces

Any natural surface can be used for pyrography, including wood, gourds, paper-mache, cotton and linen cloth, watercolor paper, and vegetable-tanned leather. Avoid any material that has been chemically treated or painted, because the high temperatures of the tool tips will release the chemical fumes of these materials during the burning process.

WOOD

Basswood and poplar are favorite woods for pyrographers. Both species have finely packed wood grain and a naturally pale white coloration, and both are commonly available in ⅛" (3mm) or thicker plywood sheets. The natural color of wood affects the color ranges that you will be able to see in your work. Naturally pale basswood, poplar, and birch will show a very wide range of pale-toned burns. Dark African mahogany and black walnut will not show burning until you reach mid-toned or dark-toned burns.

VEGETABLE-TANNED LEATHER

Vegetable-tanned, non-dyed leather is a favorite burning medium. Pyrography leather is available in large pieces, pre-cut kits, and manufactured forms such as purses, book covers, and wallets. Leather offers the pyrographer a world of three-dimensional possibilities.

Leather comes in a variety of weights, from very lightweight 1-ounce leather, which is approximately ¹⁄₆₄" (0.4mm) thick, to 8-ounce leather at ⅛" (3mm) thick, and even heavier belt-weight leather that can be as thick as ¼" (6mm).

Leather is also available in pre-dyed colors and suede textures, neither of which are recommended for burning: the chemicals used to create dyed leathers can produce toxic fumes during the burning process, and textured suede does not provide a smooth, uniform surface for clean, clear burned lines.

GOURDS

Dried craft gourds make wonderful surfaces for your pyrography projects. Dried gourds, with their densely packed, woodlike fibers, provide an artist with interesting shapes for their pattern decoration. Easily cut with a craft knife or bench knife, a gourd can become a bowl, sand candle cup, vase, lamp, or, of course, delightful birdhouse. Use a dust mask when cleaning and cutting any dried craft gourd, because gourds often have fine powder residue surrounding the inner seed pod that can cause both skin and lung irritation.

In this burning, worked on 8-ounce vegetable-tanned leather, the landscape structures are used as a pale background scene to provide the setting for an old truck and car.

ARTIST-QUALITY PAPERS

Artists use many styles of paper for their work in watercolors, marker illustration, pastels, and hand-pulled prints. The heavyweight, high-quality papers used for these arts are suitable for any pyrography pattern. You can find these papers with anything from a very smooth surface to a deeply toothed (or pebbly) texture. For pyrography, a smooth or lightly textured surface works best, since the pebbling can distort your lines as you burn. Paper is an interesting pyrography medium because you can easily color your designs with colored pencils, pastels, inks, and watercolors when you have finished burning.

PAPER-MACHE AND CHIPBOARD

Both chipboard and paper-mache are made from shredded paper pulp. The pulp can be pressed into strong, flat sheets called chipboard or pressed into a mold to create three-dimensional shapes. Undyed chipboard is available in a natural medium gray-beige tone, which limits your tonal value range in the pale value areas. You can also purchase chipboard that has a polished, white paper coating.

Transferring Patterns

Two products that you can use to transfer a design to your work surface are carbon paper and graphite paper, which are both types of transfer paper.

Lay transfer paper under your paper pattern so that the transfer side is against your work surface. Then start tracing the paper pattern with a pencil or pen. As you trace, the transfer paper will deposit a fine line on

Medium-textured, 140-pound watercolor paper is an inexpensive and extremely versatile medium for pyrography.

your work surface. Any transfer paper should be used carefully, as the transfer lines cannot be easily removed from your work surface after the burning is complete. I tend to use graphite paper most often because of its pale gray coloring, especially on gourds, paper-mache, and darker woods.

You can also create your own homemade transfer paper. Blacken the back of a pattern paper with a soft pencil, covering the back completely. Place the pattern onto your work surface and trace over the pattern lines just as you would with real transfer paper. This will leave a fine line of pencil graphite on your work surface. Pencil rubbing tracings leave extremely fine, thin lines, which are accurate to your tracing, easy to follow, and easy to clean up with a white artist eraser after burning.

Pencil rubbing pattern transfer.

Graphite paper pattern transfer.

Carbon paper pattern transfer.

Safety

Before beginning any pyrography project or practice, you must be familiar with a few simple safety guidelines.

1. Your project medium should be an untreated, unpainted, and unfinished natural surface. Paints, polyurethane sealers, varnishes, and chemicals used in treating wood can release toxic fumes during the burning process.
2. Search online to double-check that the medium you will be burning does not have any toxic properties. There are several excellent databases available. For some suggestions, see page 206.
3. Work in a well-ventilated area. A small fan placed on your table can move the smoke and fumes away from your face. Whenever possible, work near an open window.
4. Avoid placing your project in your lap while burning. This places your face directly above the fumes, increasing your chances of inhaling the smoke.
5. Unplug your burning unit from the wall socket whenever you are not working. A moment of forgetfulness and an unattended hot pen tip can cause a fire.
6. While working, set your pens either on the pen stand provided by the manufacturer or on a ceramic tile to protect your work surface.

Finishing Sealers

The lines and shading that you work with your burning tools do not require a finishing sealer. They are permanently set into the work surface. However, your work surface may need a finishing coat to seal the project from dirt, to give the completed project a shine, or to protect any paint or pencil coloring you add to your burning.

Cotton cloth and paper are usually not sealed after the work is completed. Vegetable-tanned leather may need a waterproof coating of oil added. Wood often needs a finishing coat of spray sealer, varnish, or oil finish.

Polyurethane and acrylic spray sealers are readily available and easy to use. After any painting steps are completely dry, apply two to three light coats, allowing each coat to dry thoroughly. This type of sealer coat comes in matte, semi-matte, and gloss sheens and does not change the natural color of your wood.

An oil finish, such as tung oil, Danish oil, or a half-and-half mix of turpentine and linseed oil, gives a soft sheen to your work. Apply oils following the manufacturer's directions. Dispose of any oil-coated rags or paper towels only after submerging them in soapy water—oily rags are a fire hazard. Oil finishes darken the tonal value of the wood, and so will change or darken your pyrography work.

Brush-on polyurethane and varnishes are also available for your pyrography project at your local hardware store. Follow the manufacturer's directions and allow ample time between coats for thorough drying. Polyurethane does not change the natural coloring of your wood and gives a very durable long-term finish. Varnishes, however, can give the wood a golden-yellow cast. Do a small test sample on a scrap board to check the final varnish coloring. Like polyurethane, varnishes give a strong, lasting protective coating to your work.

"Grandpa's Pride," worked on a 12" (30cm) square birch plywood board and finished with a polyurethane spray semi-gloss sealer.

Wood Patina

Wood naturally changes color with age, developing a darker tonal value patina. White pine, which has a very clear, white coloring when freshly cut, becomes a deep golden yellow within a decade. Birch and basswood, both common pyrography woods, darken to a soft taupe or beige-brown coloring.

As the wood ages, it can appear that your pyrography work is fading. Your palest tonal values can become completely lost as the wood naturally darkens, overpowering your pale and pale-medium coloration. Unfortunately, you cannot stop wood from aging. However, you can take several easy precautions to minimize the effects of aging:

The only difference between the two burned samples shown here is that the right-hand project, "Country Church," is about fifteen years older than the left-hand project, "After the Rain." The birch plywood of "Country Church" has developed a deep golden patina over the years.

- Check what color changes your wood will develop before you begin your project. If your wood will darken dramatically over time, work your burning in strong mid-medium to black-dark tones, avoiding the pale tonal range.
- Use a sealer that provides UV light protection. This reduces the oxidation that causes wood to develop a patina. Do not display or hang your work in full sunlight to avoid UV light changes.
- Avoid using oil finishes on woods that naturally have dark patinas. As an example, birch plywood can take on a soft beige tone when coated with Danish oil finish or tung oil. It naturally develops a deeper beige tone through aging patina. These two factors can totally block out your mid-tone values within a few years.

"Country Church," above right, was burned in 2001 for my book *Great Book of Woodburning*. "After the Rain," above left, was burned in 2017. You can compare the tonal values of the pyrography work to see that the burning remains strong. What has changed between these two birch plywood pieces is just the golden patina that "Country Church" has developed in the sixteen-year period.

Correcting Mistakes

Everyone occasionally makes a mistake while working on pyrography projects. There are several methods to change or correct an area in your burning.

The easiest and quickest method is to **reburn the area with a higher temperature setting and more densely packed texture** to block out your error. This can cover up a misburned line or disguise an area in your work. If you darken the value of an area, be sure to adjust all of the surrounding shading to compensate for this deeper tone. You may need to reshade well beyond the original error area.

The second common method used to correct mistakes is to **remove the error using a woodcarving tool**. A straight chisel, bull nose chisel, or large round gouge can be used to cut away the upper layer of wood, exposing a clean, unburned surface. Use as shallow a carving stroke as possible to do this. Lightly sand the area of the carving cut using 220- to 320-grit sandpaper to smoothly grade the cut into the surrounding intact area. Then proceed to reburn the area.

2 | All About Pen Tips

Each pen tip creates its own unique line patterns. Line writing tips like ball tips and looped tips burn thin lines for detailing, touch-and-lift dot patterns for solid fills, and the scrubbie stroke for medium tonal value fills. Flat and curved spear shaders burn wide, graduated shading strokes, perfect for wood grain textures and leaf cluster patterns. Square wire shaders, created with heavy-gauge triangular wire, are used to create fine blades of grass, animal hair and fur, and barn board detailing. The pen tip you use can determine the art style of your finished pyrography. In this chapter, we will look in depth at the five basic pen tip profiles and the stroke patterns each make, as well as correct hand position for maximum comfort and best results.

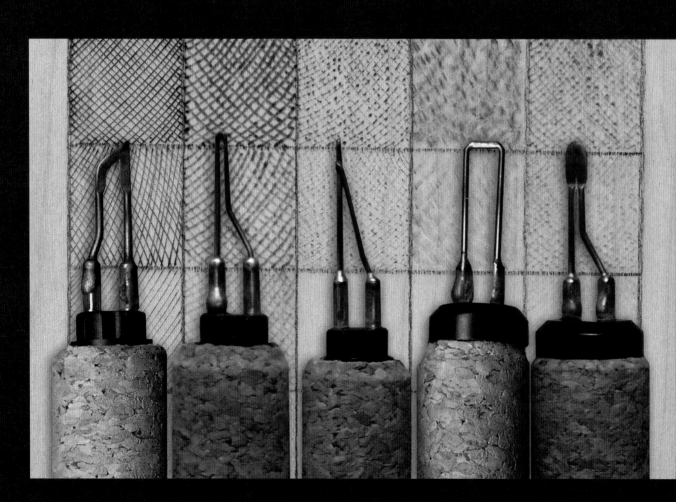

Pen Tips

Each pen tip creates its own width and shape of line burn, and therefore is more suitable for specific textures. Thin-edged, flat spear shaders or curved spear shaders cut thin, deep lines. Line writing tips, like ball tips and looped tips, burn thick, shallow lines. A basic beginner's set of tips may include a looped tip, a ball tip, a flat spear shader, a curved spear shader, and a square wire shader. These five tips will allow you to burn a vast variety of projects. Specialty tips can be added as you discover your own personal style of burning. Tip shapes and names vary depending on the manufacturer, and the tips are often offered in several sizes. Please check the website for your unit for more specific tips that are available for your use.

Variable-temperature pens come in two varieties: fixed pens and interchangeable pens. A fixed pen has the burning wire permanently set into the pen. An interchangeable pen allows different types of tip to be inserted into the end of the pen. Interchangeable pens allow you to purchase a wider variety of burning tips, which is a great advantage to the new pyrographer.

Each manufacturer creates their pens to specifically fit the electric voltage, wire, and connections used in their burning units. Although some manufacturers do sell conversion kits that allow you to use pens manufactured by other companies on their units, I do not recommend this practice. Using another company's pens can void your warranty and can damage both your pens and your burning unit.

When you purchase your variable-temperature unit, consider not only the power features of the unit but also the pen construction, how the pens connect to the unit, the guard grip construction, and the variety of tip profiles available for your unit. See more info about burning units on pages 7–8.

The first three tips are fixed pens and the last two pens are interchangeable pens (all Colwood brand). The interchangeable tips are secured in a plug-in male connector that snaps into the top of the pen, giving an even, reliable temperature for your burning. From left: curved spear shader, looped tip, micro looped tip, square wire shader, and flat spear shader.

These Optima 1 Dual tips are all fixed pens. From left: curved spear shader, flat spear shader, and ball tip.

LINE WRITING TIP: BALL TIP

There are two kinds of line writing tips: ball tips and looped tips (see page 17). Ball tips come in a variety of diameters, with larger-diameter tips creating wider lines and smaller-diameter tips creating thinner lines. They have three primary purposes: outlining and writing, scrubbie shading, and solid fill textures.

Outlining and Writing

You can outline all of your pattern lines to give your piece a cartoon, coloring book, or abstract art effect. To do this, first lightly outline the pattern using a cool temperature setting to set your lines. Next, work each area with your chosen style or texture. Then, when all of the shaded texture work is done, rework the outlines at a medium-high to high setting. Vary the width of the lines to give your outlining more interest.

Not every project needs to be outlined, though. If you work your project using shaded tonal values, outlines will not be needed to visually separate one area from another. No object in nature comes with a true outline. For realistic landscape scenes or animal portraits, use as few outlines as possible.

Scrubbie Shading

Small, short "scrubbie" strokes can be made with a ball tip to create evenly graduated shading for your elements. Scrubbies are made in a slow, even, back-and-forth motion or in a tight, random, circular movement. Work several layers of scrubbie strokes to deepen the tonal value in any area. In the car image, scrubbie strokes are used to add shading around the wheel and elsewhere.

Solid Fill Textures

Medium to medium-high temperature settings and a touch-and-lift stroke using a ball tip will create solid fill areas comprised of lots of little dots. The more tightly you pack the small, dark dots, the darker your area will be. Avoid using a high temperature setting for this type of fill texture, though, as a very hot setting will cause the dots to bleed or halo into the adjacent areas of the design.

Outlining

Scrubbie stroke shading

Touch-and-lift dot fill

LINE WRITING TIP: LOOPED TIP

Along with the ball tip, the looped tip is a kind of line writing tip. This classic pen tip is a mainstay for any tool kit. The tightly bent loop at the point of the tip creates even, medium-width lines and carries the heat for your burning unit well.

Fine Line Work

Using any temperature setting and holding the tip almost perpendicular to the wood, you can make even lines for shading, accents, and outline work. The higher you set your temperature, the darker and thicker the lines will burn. In the photo at top right, the fine line work is used to shade under the roof overhang. By reburning the lines, the tonal value can be darkened.

Texture Patterns

Any texture pattern can be created using a looped tip. Simple random curls, tightly packed circles, and crosshatched patterns are easily made using the fine line of the looped tip. The more tightly you pack any texture line, the darker the tonal value that area will have.

Solid Fill Textures

At high temperature settings, you can use the looped tip to create tightly packed, small ovals to bring an area into your darkest tonal value. In the photo at bottom right, this touch-and-lift stroke is used to establish the darkest shadows for the leaves.

Fine lines and detailing

Texture fill

Touch-and-lift solid fill

FLAT SPEAR SHADER

Spear shaders have a flattened surface that may be rounded or pointed at the tip. The shaft of the tip is bent so that the flat of the shader lies fully against the wood. Flat spear shaders, sometimes called spoon shaders, tend to have a thicker metal tip than curved spear shaders (see page 19), so they may require a slightly higher temperature setting during use.

Scrubbie Shading

By setting the temperature to medium or medium-high, you can lay the flat of the shader against the wood and pull short, gentle strokes across the wood to create a soft scrubbie shading effect. Lifting the shader slightly to work the tip closer to the edge allows you to move in a random, circular motion for even shading. Add multiple layers of shading strokes to graduate an area from a pale to dark tonal value.

Leading Edge Lines

In the photo at right, the flat spear shader is used twice to create the cupola boards. The shader is first laid flat against the wood and pulled in a long, straight line to give the general shape of the boards. A second stroke is then laid over the long stroke to separate each board with a fine, thin, slightly darker tone by leaning the shader's side edge into the wood.

Touch and Lift Shading

The shape of the flat spear shader is perfect for a simple triangular touch-and-lift stroke. In the photo at bottom right, a pine tree is created by laying the tip of the shader on the outside edge of the tree branches; this makes the tips of the branches darker than the inner branch areas.

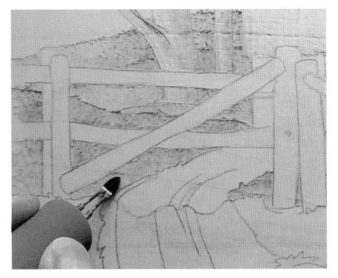

Flat-to-wood scrubbie shading

Leading edge lines

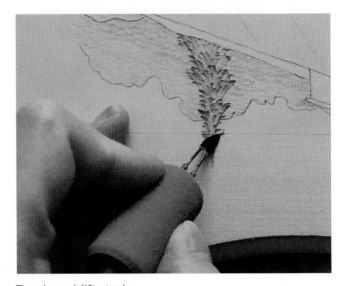

Touch-and-lift stroke

CURVED SPEAR SHADER

The curved spear shader has a thinner metal body than the flat spear shader (see page 18), which allows it to create darker tonal values at lower temperature settings. The curved side makes even lines without a dark starting point spot, as often happens with a ball tip (see page 16).

Long Shading Strokes

Using the wide point in the curve—the belly—you can pull long, wide shading strokes. In the photo at top right, these long strokes are used to create the dips and ruts in an old country road. This is a touch-and-slowly-pull movement.

Fine Line Work

Leading with the point of the curved spear shader and rolling into the belly creates extremely thin, fine lines. On low temperature settings, these lines are barely visible. On hotter settings, the lines are perfect for engraving, cross-hatching, and accent work. In the photo at right, the edge of the belly of the shader is used to create the line work in the dirt road. Note that some of the lines are so pale that they only show because of the natural shadow of the cut line.

Triangles

Because the curved spear shader carries a large amount of heat, the tip of this shader can create small, evenly sized triangles in your designs. Set your thermostat on a medium or medium-hot setting and use a touch-and-lift stroke. The lower you hold the shader to the wood, the larger your triangle will be. In the photo at bottom right, these small triangles are used to create the rotted, uneven edge of the barn boards.

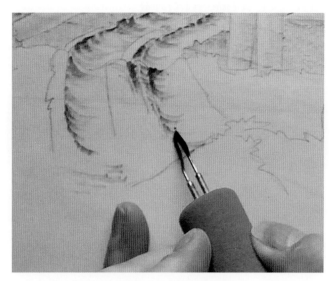

Using the belly for long shading strokes

Using the point for detailing lines

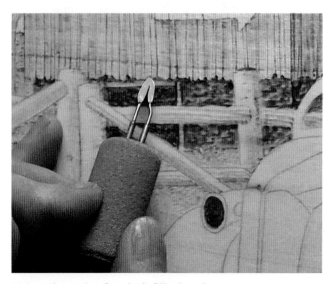

Using the point for dark fill triangles

SQUARE WIRE SHADER

The square wire shader is a specialty tip that is a joy to use. The wide leading edge of this shader fills areas quickly with bold strokes. It is a must for any large-format project and will save you hours of work filling or shading a design.

Because the leading edge is straight, you can hold the pen perpendicular to the work and, using a touch-and-lift stroke, make perfectly straight, short lines. Lay a metal-edged ruler against your project and glide the pen tip along the ruler to create long, perfect line work. (Metal rulers will drain some of the heat from your pen tip, so adjust your temperature setting to a slightly higher setting as needed).

The square wire shader shown in the photo at top right is made with a triangular wire, making it perfect for animal hair and long, flowing grass blades. With a square wire shader that is made with a round wire, you can lead one point of the straight edge into your wood, creating a thick to thin straight line.

Short, perfect shader lines

Hand Position

No matter which pen and tip you are using, your hand position controls the pressure on the tip, the length of the stroke, and the curvature of the burned line.

Any pen is held loosely, as if you were holding a writing pen or pencil on its grip. On the pen shown on page 17, the grip guard is a long cork layer. On the pens shown on this page, the grip guard is a fat blue foam layer. These are two typical grip guards you will find on pens, and they help keep your fingers from sliding down too close to the hot tips.

A loose grip between the thumb and index finger places the tip at roughly a 45-degree angle to your work. You can raise the angle to create a thinner line burn, and you can lower the angle to create a wider burn line.

Avoid resting the side of your hand on your project, as this restricts your hand movements and shortens your strokes. I lightly rest my small finger on the project; this balances my hand and secures the pen tip in a specific position on the board.

Hold your burning pen exactly as you would any writing tool. A comfortable hand position makes clean, easy burn strokes.

CHAPTER

3 | Creating Essential Practice Boards

In this chapter, we will discuss the importance of creating a practice board, learn how to mark the grid work for texture fills, and review examples of pen tip strokes that you can use in your projects.

Creating a practice board before you begin your project allows you to test your tip points, experiment with your temperature settings, and explore the textures that you can use on any pyrography project. Over time, your practice boards will become a library of ideas and possibilities that you can use on new projects.

If you are starting a new project, work your practice session on the same medium on which you will burn your design. I often add small portions of my project pattern to my practice board to discover how I want to handle that area of the work before I go to my final project.

Comparing Temperature Settings and Woods

The three practice boards shown here were worked in the same burning session using three different burning units and three different species of wood: poplar, basswood, and birch. You can see that each wood develops its tonal values at a different temperature setting and has its own range of possible values. I strongly recommend that you create a similar practice board using your burning unit and mark the temperature settings that you used to reach the different tonal values. Prepare the board first following steps 1–2 of Basic Board Preparation on page 25. (In all three practice boards, the left column was burned with the Walnut Hollow Versa-Tool, the center column with the Colwood Detailer, and the right column with the Optima 1 Dual unit.)

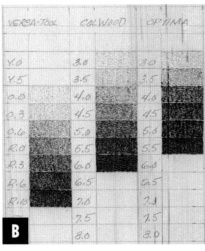

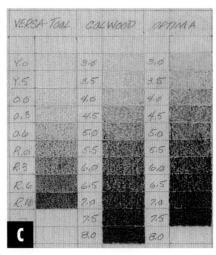

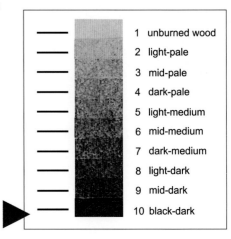

Poplar (A) is a very soft wood that burns to dark tones at low and medium settings, which can limit the number of tonal values you can establish. **Basswood (B)** is a fine-grained white wood that is readily available to the crafter in premade shapes like plaques, plates, and frames. **Birch (C)** is a tight-grained hardwood that is most readily available to the crafter as ⅛" (3mm) to ¼" (6mm) plywood. The hardness of the wood allows for a very wide range of tonal values.

Creating a Tonal Value Reference Scale

The wood species, tip, texture stroke, density of line work, and temperature setting of your burning unit combine to determine your tonal values. Because so many factors come into play, I cannot give you specific temperature setting numbers for your unit or for the wood that you are working.

Therefore, to establish a scale for your use while referring to content in this book, I will refer to all tonal value settings by using the tonal value scale at right. Before you begin any step-by-step projects in this book, please work a similar 10-unit tonal value scale on your own practice board

This is the tonal value scale used to note the temperature setting throughout the projects in this chapter. ▶

1 unburned wood
2 light-pale
3 mid-pale
4 dark-pale
5 light-medium
6 mid-medium
7 dark-medium
8 light-dark
9 mid-dark
10 black-dark

so that you know what actual temperature settings you need to use to achieve each value. Prepare the board first following steps 1–2 of Basic Board Preparation on page 25.

The first unit of your scale, your palest tonal value, is the color of the unburned wood. Use the simple scrubbie stroke (see page 16) to fill each subsequent tonal unit, slowly developing your range from light-pale through black-dark. With a pencil, mark your practice board with the temperature setting that your unit used to create each tonal value. Then print a copy of this page on a high-ink setting, and note on it your temperature settings for each tonal value. As you work through the projects in this book, you can refer to your paper chart and your practice board to accurately copy the tonal value work in your project.

Creating a Tonal Value Window

Tonal values in a photograph or in a finished burning can sometimes be deceptive when it comes to exactly how light or dark they are along the tonal value scale. A mid-tone burn may appear much darker than it really is if it lies directly against an extremely pale tonal value. That same mid-tone burn can also appear lighter than its true value if set against a very dark or black area of burning.

To eliminate the effects of the adjacent tonal values so that you can determine the exact tonal range of an area, you can create a tonal value window as shown here. Print a copy of this tonal value scale, then cut out the narrow, long rectangle of paper just to the right of the scale.

To use the window, lay it directly onto your photograph or burning. Adjust the position of the

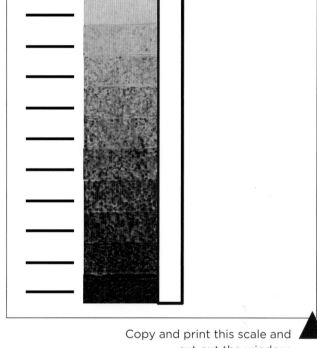

Copy and print this scale and cut out the window.

cutout so that you can see the area that you are working through the window. Now adjust the window, moving it up or down, until the tonal value of the photo matches one of the tonal values printed on the scale. The window lets you see just the area that you are working, blocking out the surrounding areas that can affect how you perceive that particular area.

Place the window over the area you are burning to check the accurate tonal value.

Creating a Grayscale Window

Images that are grayscale, like black and white photos or pencil drawings, can easily be translated into standard tonal values (and their corresponding temperature settings) by using the double-scale window shown here. This window has the sepia standard tonal value scale on the left side and the grayscale equivalent on the right. The window area falls between the two scales. You can position the paper window over the relevant area of the photo you are referencing and adjust the window until the grayscale value of the area matches one of the grayscale values on the paper window. The corresponding sepia tonal value scale gives you the tonal value and temperature setting for your actual burning work.

Copy and print this scale and cut out the window. ▶

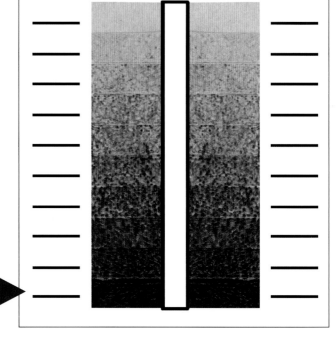

Place the window over the area you are referencing to discover the sepia tonal value.

Basic Board Preparation

These basic instructions will apply to virtually any project or practice board you do. Simply choose your piece of wood, then prepare it using the following tools and steps as applies to your particular project.

SUPPLIES

- 220-grit or 320-grit sandpaper
- 6" to 8" (15cm to 20cm) square of heavy brown kraft paper (or paper grocery bag)
- Painter's tape or low-tack masking tape
- Pattern printed on chosen pattern transfer paper or white paper (see page 11)
- #4 to #8 soft artist's pencil (if using white paper for pattern transfer)
- Hard pencil or pen
- White artist's eraser
- Ruler

1 Sand the wood. Prepare your wood by lightly sanding the entire surface using 220-grit or finer sandpaper. Work the sanding with the grain of the wood to avoid creating small, circular swirl lines that can show later as the burning develops. Wipe the board with a clean, dry cloth to remove any dust.

2 Rub the wood. Crumple the brown kraft paper in your hands to create a crushed ball. Rub the ball over the wood. This kind of paper makes wonderfully fine sandpaper, leaving your wood smooth and even. Wipe the board with a clean, dry cloth to remove any dust.

3 Prepare the pattern. If you are using a pattern, choose the pattern transfer method that you prefer for your project (more info on page 11) and prepare your pattern accordingly.

4 Measure the board. Measure the wood to determine the center point of each edge of the board. Connect each center point by lightly drawing one vertical line and one horizontal line through the middle of the wood.

5 Transfer the pattern. Fold your pattern into quarters, first folding along the vertical axis and then folding along the horizontal axis. Unfold your pattern and match the fold lines of the pattern to the pencil lines on your wood. Tape the pattern into place, then trace the entire pattern firmly with a hard pencil or pen. Check the quality of the tracing before you completely remove the pattern paper.

Quilt Barn Texture Practice Board

The barn scene on the right of this practice board was worked using texture fills to create both the line work and tonal value shadings. After transferring the pattern to the wood, you simply fill each area of the pattern with a repetitive texture stroke. This practice board will teach you how easy it is to create tons of textures using just a few basic pen tips, and allow you to try your hand at applying textures somewhere other than practice squares.

SUPPLIES

- 9" x 11" (23 x 28cm) birch plywood
- Pen tips: ball tip, looped tip, flat spear shader, curved spear shader
- All basic board preparation supplies (see page 25)
- Pattern on page 157

PREPARING THE BOARD

1 Prepare. Prepare your board following the Basic Board Preparation instructions on page 25, but wait to transfer the actual Quilt Barn pattern until step 2 of these instructions.

2 Outline. Using a pencil and ruler, mark a ½" (1cm) margin on all sides of the board, then mark the texture practice area in nine rows of five 1" (2.5cm) squares. In the remaining rectangular area on the right side of the board, transfer the Quilt Barn Texture Practice Board pattern (page 157).

3 Practice. Following the numbered guide and the detailed instructions on the following pages, work through each grid square. Then work the textures into the actual barn pattern on the right, following the photo for tonal value.

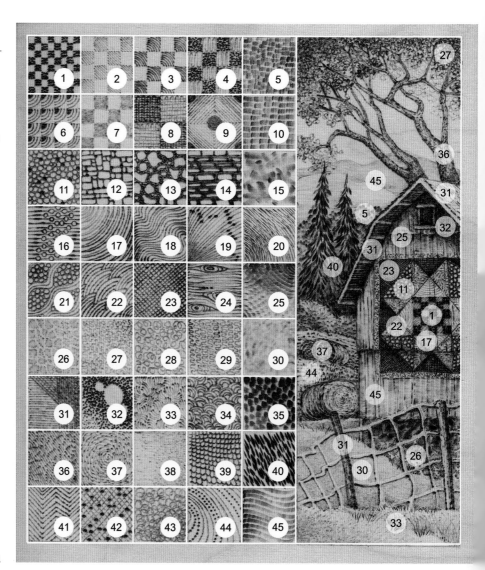

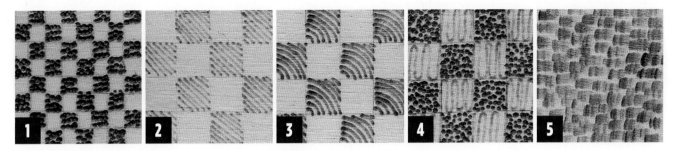

1   Ball tip, high temperature setting, checkerboard dots
2   Ball tip, low temperature setting, checkerboard straight lines
3   Looped tip, medium temperature setting, checkerboard curved lines
4   Looped tip, medium temperature setting, checkerboard dots and looped lines
5   Curved spear shader, medium temperature setting, short pull lines

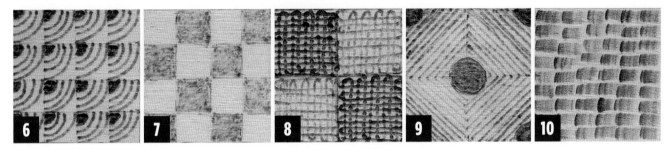

6   Ball tip, high temperature setting, curved lines
7   Ball tip, low temperature setting, tightly packed scrubbie lines
8   Looped tip, medium and high temperature settings, looped lines
9   Looped tip, graduated temperature settings, straight lines
10   Flat spear shader (on flat), medium temperature setting, pull stroke

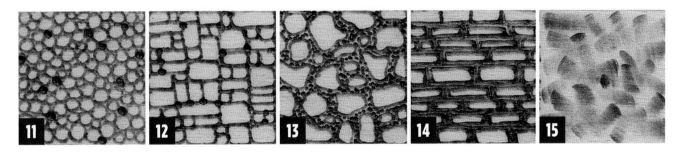

11   Looped tip, medium temperature setting, small open circles and dots
12   Looped tip, medium temperature setting, bricks
13   Looped tip, medium–high temperature setting, rock path
14   Looped tip, high temperature setting, stone wall
15   Curved spear shader (on flat), high temperature setting, random pull stroke

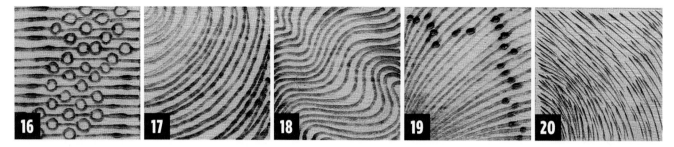

16   Looped tip, high temperature setting, lines and bubbles
17   Looped tip, graduated temperature settings, connected curved lines
18   Ball tip, medium temperature setting, wavy lines
19   Ball tip, medium temperature setting, curved lines with dots
20   Curved spear shader (on point), high temperature setting, short curved lines

21   Ball tip, medium temperature setting, bubbles and wavy lines
22   Ball tip, medium temperature setting, interlocking curves
23   Flat spear shader (on edge), medium temperature setting, cross-hatching
24   Looped tip, high temperature setting, wood grain knots
25   Flat spear shader (on flat), high temperature setting, wood grain texture

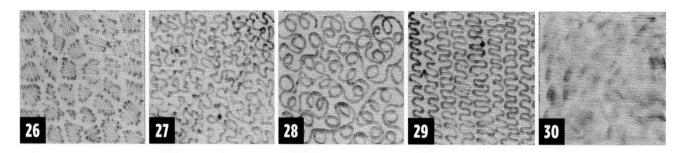

26   Curved spear shader (on point), medium temperature setting, giraffe spots
27   Ball tip, medium temperature setting, random doodle lines
28   Ball tip, medium temperature setting, looped lines
29   Ball tip, medium temperature setting, bedsprings
30   Flat spear shader (on flat), medium temperature setting, random line shading

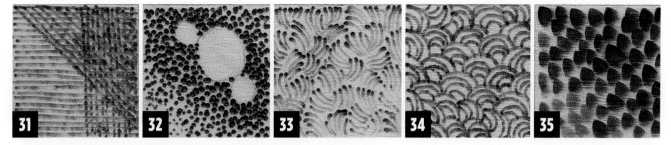

31 Looped tip, medium temperature setting, cross-hatching
32 Looped tip, medium temperature setting, variably spaced dots
33 Looped tip, medium temperature setting, grass seed heads
34 Looped tip, medium temperature setting, random shells
35 Flat spear shader (on flat), high temperature setting, touch-and-lift dashes

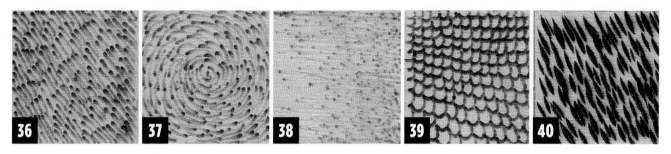

36 Flat spear shader (on point), medium temperature setting, short straight dashes
37 Flat spear shader (on point), medium temperature setting, short curved dashes
38 Flat spear shader (on point), low temperature setting, graduated dashes
39 Ball tip, medium temperature setting, dragon scales
40 Flat spear shader (on edge), high temperature setting, touch-and-lift dashes

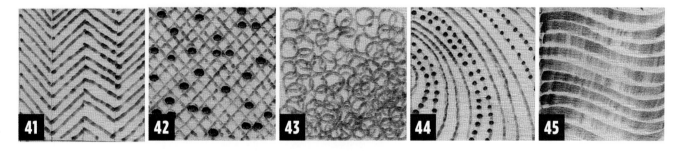

41 Ball tip, medium temperature setting, herringbone lines
42 Ball tip, medium and high temperature settings, dot-filled cross-hatching
43 Ball tip, low temperature setting, overlapping circles
44 Ball tip, medium and high temperature settings, crop circles
45 Curved spear shader (on flat), high temperature setting, long slow-pull lines

Architectural Elements Practice Board

Whether you are burning a country barn, a village church, or a house, you will discover that you can use one pattern to achieve many different looks by simply changing the architectural elements from which the building is created. This practice board is a great way to learn how to burn many of the most common building materials.

SUPPLIES

- 12" (30cm) square basswood or birch plywood
- Pen tips: ball tip, looped tip, flat spear shader, curved spear shader, square wire shader
- All basic board preparation supplies (see page 25)

PREPARING THE BOARD

1 **Prepare.** Prepare your board following the Basic Board Preparation instructions on page 25, but skip the pattern transfer steps.

2 **Outline.** Using a pencil and ruler, mark guidelines across the board to create a rectangular grid with 14 total working areas of approximately 1½" x 2½" (4 x 6cm).

3 **Practice.** Following the detailed descriptions on the following pages, try to imitate the different realistic building materials shown.

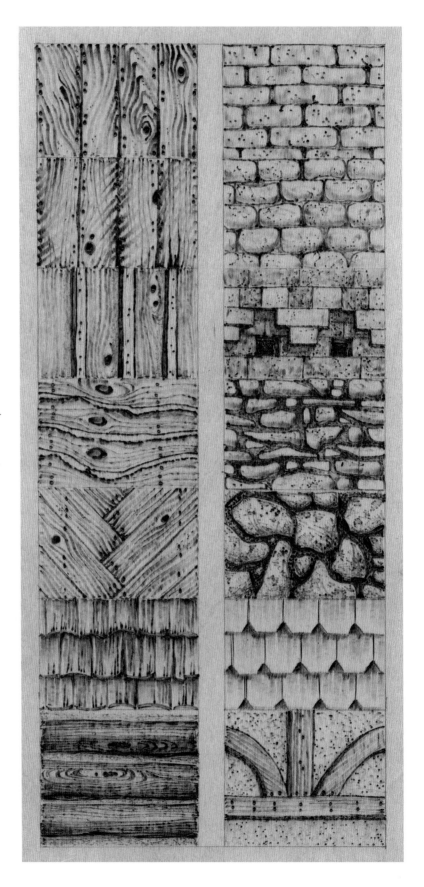

Milled boards, with age, begin to show their distinct grain lines with deeper tonal values in some areas of the grain. This style of wall construction butts the long edge of each board tightly against its neighbor.

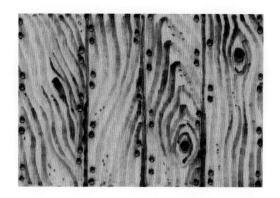

Hand-sawn boards will show the curves of the saw work crossing over the grain of the wood. Work the wood grain first using a flat spear shader or curved spear shader, then add the saw marks over the grain lines. In this style of board construction, there can be small, open gaps between the board joints.

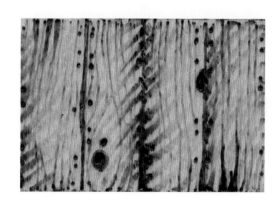

Board and batten construction uses a small, thin board over the joint lines of the larger wall boards. These small boards, the batten boards, are raised above the surface of the main wall structure and used to seal the main board joints from rainwater.

Saw mills may sell their end trims or top trims from cut logs for **siding**. These boards often have curved, wavy edges and some bark left along one long side of the board. The boards are laid onto the wall from the bottom up, with the bark edge of one board overlapping the board below.

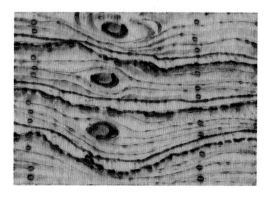

Both milled and hand-sawn boards can be nailed to the wall in **patterns**, as this diagonal design shows. Often this is worked on the side of the barn that faces the main road. The other walls of the barn may or may not be laid in the same manner.

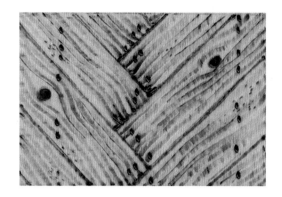

The classic **log cabin** style of construction alternates one full log on the front and back of the structure, then one full log on the two sides. Where the logs cross on the corners, the intersection area will be cut either flat or with a curve that matches the supporting log to lock each log into place. This style of construction leaves a gap between each log on the sides of the barn. After all of the walls have been created, the worker packs the spaces between the logs with mortar, cob, or even sod.

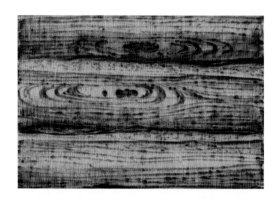

Split shingles can be used on both the wall construction and the roofs of your barn structures. The splits are cut at a taper with the thick end at the bottom edge—the overlapping edge—of the shingle, and the thinner edge at the top, where it will be covered by another shingle. Shingles are laid row by row with the top row shingle covering the intersection of two shingles on the row below. Wood shingles often cup or warp with age. This makes a fun and interesting wavy line across each of the shingle rows.

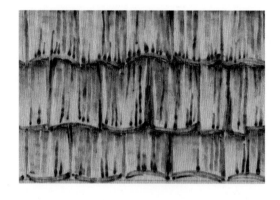

Slate roofs are laid in the same manner as split shingle roofs. Two holes are drilled in the top of the slate rectangle, in which a nail may be driven into the roof underlayment to hold the shingle in place. Slate and shingles can be hand-cut or factory-cut to make each shingle uniform in size and to create different end patterns along the bottom edge of the shingle. Different end patterns can be used to create a decorative pattern in the placement of your shingle and slate roof work.

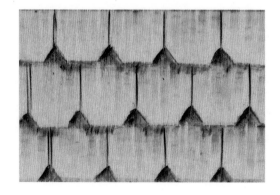

Hand-formed clay bricks or mud and dab cobs vary greatly in their general shape, size, and texture. Cob is a combination of clay, straw, and manure that is worked into a small, tight loaf. The cob is then placed on top of the wall, packed into place, and allowed to dry naturally. Many cob walls are packed until the wall is fairly smooth and then covered with a thin layer of mud. Other walls may show the individual cob loaves.

Mold-packed bricks are made by forcing the clay by hand into wooden molds. The excess clay at the top of the mold is then scraped off to level the brick. The clay is then allowed to dry enough to remove the bricks from the mold, and after further drying is kiln fired. This type of brick often shows a wide range of texture because of the packing process. While the bricks will generally be the same size and shape, there will be some variation between each brick.

Step-by-Step Mold-Packed Bricks

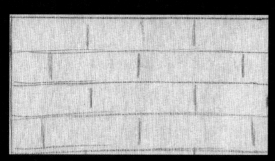

1 Draw a basic brick grid with pencil.

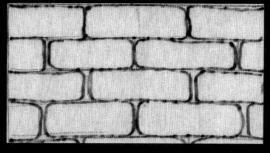

2 Burn the rounded brick outlines.

3 Shade between the bricks and add texture dots to the bricks.

4 Add shading texture to the bricks.

Manufactured bricks are extruded into the mold to ensure that each and every brick is of matching size, shape, and color. These are fired in a kiln to give the brick lasting strength. Because these bricks are so uniform, brick layers can create interesting patterns in the wall of a barn or house. By changing where each brick is placed, whether the wide side or narrow end is shown on the face of the wall, how deeply set each brick is, and whether air spaces are left between bricks, the brick layer can use several different patterns in one wall.

Flat **field stones** are the main means of construction in areas where the crop fields must be cleared of rock and debris. Stones are stacked on top of one another, interlocking in different shapes and sizes to give the wall its strength. Mortar is used between the stone to fill the gaps and cement the individual stones into one full wall structure.

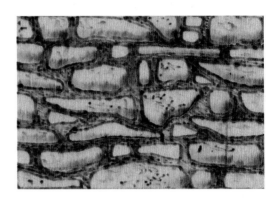

A different style of wall can be made with **large, round stones**. In this wall sample, the stones are quite smooth in texture. As with field stones, large, round stone work is held together with the use of mortar.

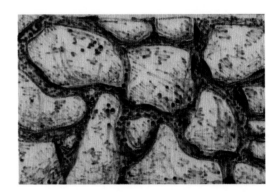

Stucco, a combination of cement, lime, and water, gives walls a rough, coarse texture that covers the entire wall surface. Wood boards may be added as decorative trim.

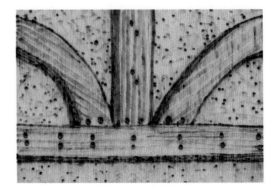

I have always believed that the better you understand your subject, the better you will be able to execute your project. Landscapes, especially farmstead, ranch, and barn scenes, have some specific elements that you need to consider to create a realistic impression with your pyrography. For maximum realism, review these elements before you begin your first landscape burnings.

TREES

Newly built barns often do not have trees within close proximity because the trees have been removed and used to build the barn. A new farm complex is marked by the clean, tree-free surroundings. Considering the large farm equipment and the movement of animals in and out of any barn complex, trees can become an impediment to a working farm. As the barn ages, small trees will sprout around the barn, usually along the walls that face away from the barn access road or in the corners or tight areas between two barn structures. So, unless the barn has been abandoned for a long period of time, you do not usually find barns located in wooded lots or even with carefully spaced, planted trees nearby.

Straight-trunked trees are only found at your local garden nursery or in thickly packed forests. The trees that may grow around your farmstead are more likely to be twisted or slanted according to where they have grown. Trees standing far from other trees or structures usually have widespread branches. Trees that are tightly packed tend to be tall and narrow. Pines tend to be along the forest edge, while deciduous trees tend to be within the main block of a forest.

CUPOLAS, ROOF VENTS, AND WALL VENTS

Most barns have one or more cupolas—a venting system along the roof ridge—to release the heat from the drying straw. Without a cupola, especially in the hotter, humid areas of the country, the straw or hay in the loft can become so hot that it can catch fire, burning the barn to the ground.

Large vent slates can be found in the peak of the barn wall; these also allow the heat and humidity of the drying hay to escape. Wood-sided barns may have very narrow, very long vent doors along the hayloft story that can be opened to allow air movement through the upper parts of the barn. Brick-walled and stone-walled barns may have openings left in the laying of the stone that allow for the barn to vent. These openings are often spaced along the wall in intriguing, repeating patterns.

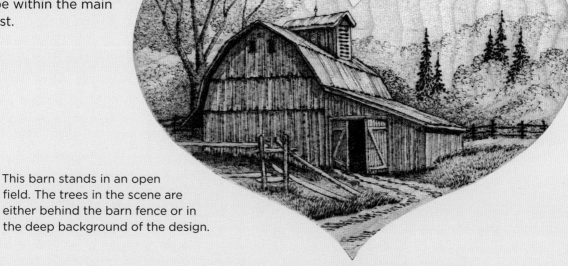

This barn stands in an open field. The trees in the scene are either behind the barn fence or in the deep background of the design.

LIGHTNING RODS

Farm complexes lie in the middle of acres and acres of tilled, cleared land that is used to grow crops or pasture animals. Because of this, the farmhouse, barn, and silos are the tallest elements in the landscape and the most likely to be hit by lightning during a storm. These structures need lightning rods along the roof ridge, and often have multiple, ornate rods.

CHIMNEYS

Any older, rural house structure in the cold, northern portion of the U.S. needs a chimney. Even in the western deserts, where the night temperatures can dramatically drop, a house may have either a chimney or a stovepipe above the roofline. The size and shape of the house determines how many chimneys one structure may have. Chimneys are built on the outside of the house or through the very center of the home, and reach above the roofline for the best draft.

ROADS AND PATHS

All dirt roads are sunken roads. Years of truck, car, and wagon traffic through rain, snow, and heat wear the road down. Roads and paths that lead into the structures of a farm complex are no different. Daily abuse by heavy equipment or moving herds of farm animals wears deep, distinct ridges and ruts into the roadbeds and often creates high dirt walls along the road edges. Houses, barns, and even springhouses have either a road or path that leads from the main farmstead structures to the building. The

This rolled-roof barn has a large cupola and three lightning rods.

road that leads to the barn will be deepest just under the barn doors. Pastures also have deeply trodden paths that are used constantly by farm animals. Remember, too, that roads lead somewhere. A road can lead your eye from the foreground to a building or can take you from the foreground to the farthest point in your landscape depth.

MAILBOXES

Adding a mailbox to your landscape is an easy way of personalizing your scene with your name, street name, or street number. But before you add a mailbox to your pattern, remember that mailboxes are always located on the main county road, never on a small side road or interior driveway on your farm. Also, mailboxes are associated with farmhouses, not barns—the residents of barns don't get mail.

FENCES, FENCE LINES, AND STONE WALLS

Old fence posts are seldom straight and square set. They can lean just a little, or can be free-hanging, supported by the fence wire. Fences are erected to either keep an animal inside the fenced area or outside of it. The fence wire is placed on the same side of the post as the animal it's meant to contain or block. That way, when a cow pushes against the fence wire, it pushes the fence against the post instead of pushing the wire off the post.

The straight edges of the top of the stairs are just enough to create a path up the sand dune to the lighthouse.

CHAPTER 4

Structure, Texture, and Weather Practice Boards

In this chapter, we will use just two patterns to teach a plethora of techniques and ideas. First, we will burn one pattern in four vastly different ways, learning how structural elements, texture, sunlight, and shadow all combine to create a realistic scene. Next, we will burn a new pattern that demonstrates how weather elements can create mood and realism. Though the projects in this chapter can be considered practice boards, they are also beautiful little vignettes in their own right, so you'll have completed full-blown projects by the time you are done.

Variation 1: Wood Board Roof Barn

This realism project focuses on using tonal value changes to define the boundary lines of each element in the pattern. We will work the burning in pale tonal value layers first to establish the general shape and shadows of the barn, cupola, silo, and trees. With more layers of shading at higher temperatures, the darker tonal values will be worked to give areas of strong contrast between the white highlighted edges and black shadows.

This barn scene uses milled boards that show the curved line of the blade as the saw is drawn through the log. The changing saw-cut lines add strong detailing to your barn structure.

SUPPLIES

- 9" x 10" (23 x 26cm) birch plywood
- Pen tips: ball tip, looped tip, flat spear shader, and curved spear shader
- Polyurethane or acrylic spray sealer
- All basic board preparation supplies (see page 25)
- Pattern on page 159

ANALYSIS: SUNLIGHT

The sunlight for the Wood Board Roof Barn comes from the 1 o'clock position, highlighting the right side of the silo, both roofs, and the front wall of the main barn structure. The shadow cast by the cupola onto the main roof shows the directional line of the rays of sunlight. This directional line also appears in the shadow cast by the left-hand side of the main barn overhang.

ANALYSIS: SHADOWS

Any sunlight source near the noon position in the sky will create intensely dark shadows along the undersides of any roof overhang areas. Note that the arrows also show that black shadows will fall on the three roofline edges that are on the left side of the barn, cupola, and silo. These thin strips of black make a striking contrast to the white highlights on the top of the roofs.

PREPARING THE BOARD

1. **Sand.** Lightly sand the board using 220- or 320-grit sandpaper. Remove any sanding dust with a clean, dry cloth (more detailed instructions in Basic Board Preparation, page 25).

2. **Mark.** Mark the outer margins of the pattern area on the board using a pencil and ruler. The t͟ margins are 1¾" (4.5cm) from the edge; the side margins are 1⅜" (3.5cm) from ͟ square area of the pattern on the board.

3. **Transfer.** Orient the board with the grain of the wood running vertically. Cen͟ board, tape it along the top edge to secure it, and transfer the design (more det͟ Board Preparation, page 25).

Structure, Texture, ͟

4 **Mask.** Cut four pieces of painter's tape. Lay the tape along the border of the traced design and lightly press into position.

Painter's tape is low-tack masking tape that will lightly adhere to your wood surface and that can be easily removed without damaging the wood fibers.

BURNING THE BOARD

5 **Map the shadow areas.** Set your temperature setting to a 4 dark-pale. Using the flat spear shader or curved spear shader, and working with the grain of the wood, use long pull strokes to begin the shading in the left barn wall, in the left cupola wall, and on the left side of the silo.

With the same temperature setting and the tool tip, burn the shadow cast by the roof's overhang in the right-side wall for both the barn and cupola.

With the light source coming into the scene from the right side, the left-side walls of the silo, barn, and cupola will be a mid-range tonal value.

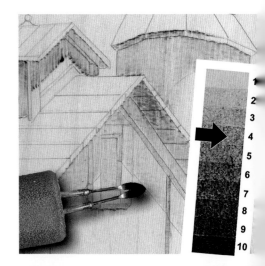

6 **Make milled barn boards.** The grain lines of the barn boards are burned using a 4 dark-pale temperature setting and either a flat spear shader or curved spear shader. Work these long pull lines over any shading done in the previous step.

The large saw blades used to cut timber into slabs often leave a semi-circular ridge on the boards. As a farmer nails the boards to the framing studs of the barn, he would alternate the direction of the boards to give more stability to his structure. In the photo, you can see how a board with the saw blade curves dipping down is laid next to a board with the curves cupping up.

Large knothole areas in a board also creates curved saw lines. Note the deeply curved saw lines in the sixth roofing board from the top.

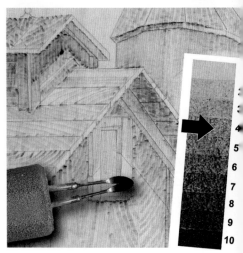

7 **Create the stone silo.** Raise your temperature to a 6 mid-medium setting. Using the ball tip or looped tip and a tightly packed short line stroke, create the large stones in the silo wall. Work the stones' line strokes directly over any previous shading.

8 **Deepen the shadows.** Using a dark-medium temperature setting and a flat spear shader or curved spear shader, strengthen the board texture strokes where the shadows fall on and from the roof overhangs.

Fill the barn wall window and along the board edges with a solid fill using a dark-medium temperature setting and a ball tip or looped tip.

Lightning rods often have a decorative metal base that is secured to the barn roof. This barn uses a simple large black ball at the bases of the rods.

9 **Detail the boards.** Using a ball tip, looped tip, or the sharp point of a curved spear shader, begin adding fine line detailing to the boards in all structures. These lines were worked at a light-dark temperature setting.

Note that the edges or outlines of the boards have not been burned. The texture strokes and tonal value changes are enough to define each element of the pattern.

10 **Develop the cupola shadows.** With a ball tip, looped tip, or curved spear shader, and a light-dark temperature setting, define the outer edges along the wood boards in the main barn structure, roof, and cupola, and on the silo roof. Allow some areas along these edges to remain unburned to give variation in your board work. Develop the boards that are used to create the cupola structure, and deepen the shading from the cupola that falls on the main barn roof.

11 **Add branches and leaves.** Lightly press painter's tape over the work already done to the barn structures in order to mask these areas from the background space.

With a dark-medium temperature setting, using the flat spear shader and short touch-and-lift strokes, create small clusters of leaves in the upper left-hand side of the pattern. Also work a small grouping of leaf clusters to the right side of the silo at the mid-point of the board. You can allow the pen tip to touch or overlap the tape to bring the leaf clusters right up to the barn roof and silo.

On the same temperature setting, using the ball tip or looped tip and a tight scrubbie stroke, fill in tree branches. Work some areas of the branches to darker tonal values than others to suggest changes in the light.

When you have completed the leaves and branches, remove the painter's tape mask.

12 **Add details.** Complete the detailing in the silo roof boards and the lightning rods, using a mid-dark setting and a ball tip or the edge of a curved spear shader.

Reinforce the blackest shadows in the pattern with a second layer of burning, following the texture strokes previously used.

Old barn boards often had major flaws that came from the sawing process or from years of weather exposure. Create these flaws using a ball tip or looped tip and a short line stroke.

13 **Finish.** Check your burning for different areas that have very similar tonal values right next to one another. As needed, reinforce one of the areas to create a stronger contrast to the adjacent element. Adjust your temperature setting as needed.

Compare the captured air space between the cupola roof, barn roof, and left silo wall. As you run your finger along the top roof edge of the barn roof, the background trees to the left and right of the cupola should feel the same.

Complete this project by erasing any remaining tracing lines with a white eraser. Remove the eraser dust with a clean, dry cloth. Apply two to three light coats of spray sealer.

Variation 2: Cedar Shingles Roof Barn

Cedar shingle roofing can be cut to any dimension, varying in width and length. For our barn, the cupola uses very small shingles, while larger-sized shingles cover the main roof of the barn. As we work through this project, the focus will be on creating the smooth, curving lines of the edges of the cedar shingles and the dark shadows that lie underneath them. Dark shadows are then used in the side edges of the shingles, in the roof overhangs, and in the background tree leaves to balance the bright, almost white tonal value of the tops of the cedar shingle roof.

Cedar shingles are a common roofing material and create a wonderful texture of cupped and curved edges along the roofline.

SUPPLIES

- 9" x 10" (23 x 26cm) birch plywood
- Pen tips: ball tip, looped tip, flat spear shader, and curved spear shader
- Pocketknife, crafting knife, utility knife, or other
- Polyurethane or acrylic spray sealer
- All basic board preparation supplies (see page 25)
- Pattern on page 160

ANALYSIS: SUNLIGHT

For this scene, the sunlight is set in the 11 o'clock position, giving the burning a late morning feeling. Note the shadowing on the right side of the silo wall—where it faces away from the light source, it is in shadow. The high position of the sun means that the cupola will cast only a small shadow onto the main roof, but the roof overhang will cast a dark, long shadow.

ANALYSIS: SHADOWS

When your light source comes from a near-overhead position, the contrast between the highlighted areas and the shadows will be intense. In this burning, you can see that there are few mid-tone or middle range values. Those shadows that are cast are in the deeper brown shades of the sepia scale, while the highlights fall in the near-white range.

PREPARING THE BOARD

1 **Sand.** Lightly sand the board using 220- or 320-grit sandpaper. Remove any sanding dust with a clean, dry cloth (more detailed instructions in Basic Board Preparation, page 25).

2 **Mask and mark.** Cover the board with one layer of painter's tape. Lightly press the tape into place. With a ruler, mark a diagonal line on the tape, working from one top corner to the opposite bottom corner. Create a second diagonal line from the remaining two corners. This marks the center point of your board. Set a compass to a radius of 3" (7.6cm) and draw a circle from the center point on the painter's tape.

3 **Cut.** Use a knife to cut along the outline of the circle. Remove the painter's tape from the circle.

4 **Transfer.** Orient the board with the grain of the wood running vertically. Center the printed pattern inside the circle, tape it along the top edge to secure it, and transfer the design (more detailed instructions in Basic Board Preparation, page 25).

5 **Add guidelines.** With a pencil and ruler, mark four evenly spaced lines across your barn roof. Mark three evenly spaced lines across the cupola roof. This delineates the separate rows of cedar shingles.

Mark a line about ½" (1cm) down from the barn window on the front wall of the barn. This will be the guideline between the two layers of siding on the wall. Two-story barns often have a dividing line of siding boards where one set of boards cover the main floor and a second layer of siding is added, overlapping the first, for the second story.

Divide the silo into four even spaces. This marks the guidelines for the board slat layers that will become the architectural element of the silo.

6 **Outline your guidelines.** Set your burning unit on a mid-pale to dark-pale tonal value temperature. Using a ball tip or looped tip, lightly outline the pattern lines.

Mark pencil guidelines on the front and side walls of the barn and on the front wall of the cupola to delineate your siding boards. Since these walls will be worked in a hand-milled or hand-cut board look, the lines do not need to be perfectly straight. Lightly burn the outline of these guidelines.

Mark in pencil where you will place your cedar shingles on each roof. Shingles are laid in an alternating pattern with the shingles in one row centered to where two shingles come together in the preceding row. Lightly burn the outline of these guidelines.

The silo is created from rows of short wood boards with a small space between each row. Create pencil guidelines for the silo siding and lightly burn the outline of these guidelines.

The side wall of the cupola is created using a lattice-work panel. Burn these lines to a mid-pale tonal value.

7 **Add the shadows.** Set your burning unit to a temperature setting for a mid-pale to dark-pale tonal value. For this step, you can use your flat spear shader, ball tip, or looped tip. All of the shading in this step is worked in thin, straight lines that run parallel to your guidelines for each area.

Burn tightly packed, thin lines on the wood siding boards in the front and side walls of the barn and in the front wall of the cupola. Using a light pressure to create a paler tonal value, burn tightly packed lines into the short board siding of the silo.

Raise the temperature setting to a dark-medium tonal value setting. Using the flat spear shader, ball tip, or looped tip, begin adding your first layers of shadows to the underside of the roof overhangs. Fill the barn window and the open spaces of the lattice of the cupola window with a solid black fill.

Because the sun is at the 11 o'clock position, the front wall of the main barn will be in a slight shadow. Use a flat spear shader to deepen the entire wall surface to a mid-medium tonal value. Repeat this for the front wall of the cupola.

8 Work the cedar shingles.
Cedar shingles can vary greatly
from each other on the same
roofline. Age and weather play
an important part in how a
cedar shingle roof will look.
Both factors cause the shingles
to cup, warp, and crack. As you
detail your shingles using a
dark-medium setting and your
ball tip or curved spear shader,
allow the edges of the shingles
to ripple across the shingle line.

Detail the side wall boards
on both the main barn and
the cupola. The silo uses metal
bands around the long side
boards, which are secured with
U-shaped bars; detail these
boards and metal bars with the
curved spear shader.

**9 Add the background tree
leaves.** With a flat spear
shader and a dark-medium
temperature setting, create the
leaves for your background
trees that fall between the
main barn and the silo. Use a
touch-and-lift stroke to create
the leaf-shaped burns.

Note that for the Wood
Board Roof Barn (page 38),
we placed the trees in the far
background of the scene, with
the silo in front of the trees.
In this scene, however, the
tree lies in the middle of the
scene, and some leaves overlap
the silo.

10 **Finish.** Remove the painter's tape mask that protected the wood surface outside of the circle of the scene. Erase any remaining tracing lines or guidelines with a white eraser. Remove the eraser dust with a clean, dry cloth. Apply two to three light coats of spray sealer.

Variation 3: Tin Roof Barn

This variation spotlights the wide variety of building materials that you can find in any old barn or farm landscape scene. We will explore how to create tin panels for the barn roof, sawn wood boards for the barn siding, smooth wood shakes (similar to shingles) for the silo roof, and ceramic tiles for the silo wall. Smooth surfaces like tin, ceramic, and sawn boards are burned using a pale to medium tonal value setting with a shader tip to work long, wide, graduated tonal lines. Note that because the materials used in this barn scene have smooth, shiny, or sanded finishes, the overall tonal value of the completed burning is much paler than the work done in the Wood Board Roof, Cedar Shingles Roof, and Thatched Roof barns. Smooth surfaces reflect light, and therefore have a tonal value setting in the pale range. To keep this pale-to-medium tonal value range throughout the work, the background tree leaves are also worked at a very pale temperature setting.

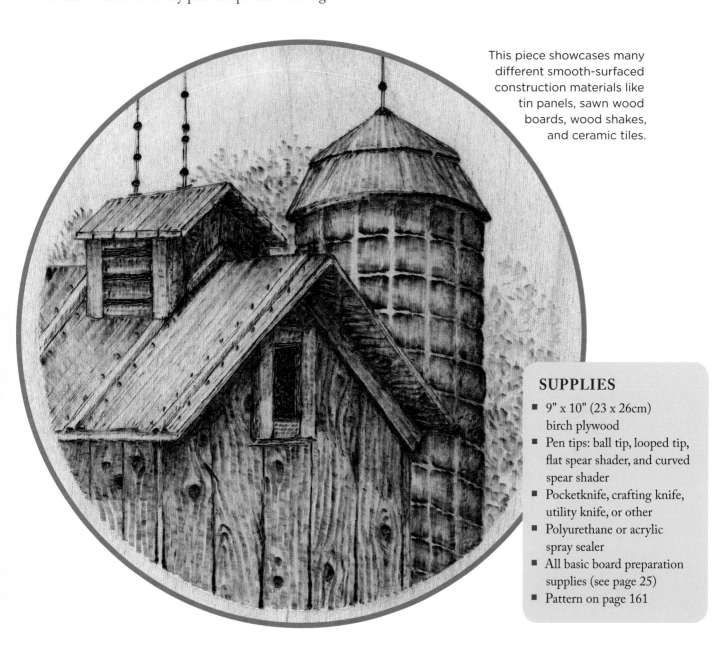

This piece showcases many different smooth-surfaced construction materials like tin panels, sawn wood boards, wood shakes, and ceramic tiles.

SUPPLIES

- 9" x 10" (23 x 26cm) birch plywood
- Pen tips: ball tip, looped tip, flat spear shader, and curved spear shader
- Pocketknife, crafting knife, utility knife, or other
- Polyurethane or acrylic spray sealer
- All basic board preparation supplies (see page 25)
- Pattern on page 161

ANALYSIS: SUNLIGHT

The long cast shadow under the left-hand roof overhang on the main barn shows that the sun is in a low, late afternoon position, perhaps between 3 and 5 p.m. This allows the shallow overhangs to create an extra-long or extra-deep shadow. There are very few direct-sun highlights; the brightest of them fall on the main roof, below the cupola, and along the center of the silo.

ANALYSIS: SHADOWS

The shadows for this barn are less dark and dramatic when compared to the higher sun position of the Wood Board Roof Barn (see page 39). Note that the underside of the wide, right-side, main barn roof is pale enough to show wood grain and individual boards.

PREPARING THE BOARD

1   **Sand.** Lightly sand the board using 220- or 320-grit sandpaper. Remove any sanding dust with a clean, dry cloth (more detailed instructions in Basic Board Preparation, page 25).

2   **Mask and mark.** Cover the board with one layer of painter's tape. Lightly press the tape into place. With a ruler, mark a diagonal line on the tape, working from one top corner to the opposite bottom corner. Create a second diagonal line from the remaining two corners. This marks the center point of your board. Set a compass to a radius of 3" (7.6cm) and draw a circle from the center point on the painter's tape.

3   **Cut.** Use a knife to cut along the outline of the circle. Remove the painter's tape from the circle.

4 **Transfer.** Orient the board with the grain of the wood running vertically. Center the printed pattern inside the circle, tape it along the top edge to secure it, and transfer the design (more detailed instructions in Basic Board Preparation, page 25). Use a ruler and pencil to create guidelines for your tin roof panels, main barn wall boards, and the tiles for the silo (like you did on page 47).

BURNING THE BOARD

5 **Burn the wood textures.** Using a flat spear shader on a dark-pale temperature setting, burn heavy wood grain lines into the boards on the main barn walls, right-side roof overhang, and cupola wall. The heavy grain and straight-cut boards imply that this barn is sided with milled white pine.

Terra cotta tiles are a common silo siding used along the east coast of the U.S. The tiles measure between 8" to 12" (20 to 30cm), and each tile varies in shades of orange, rust, and dark brown. Use the flat spear shader and the dark-pale temperature setting to shade in the silo tiles using straight vertical lines.

The tin roof on the main barn is created from flat panels that have interlocking ridges on both long sides. Use a long pull stroke, working from the top edge of the panel toward the bottom edge, to imply rust lines that develop from years of rainwater. Short, tightly packed vertical lines give the impression of a corrugated tin roof for the silo.

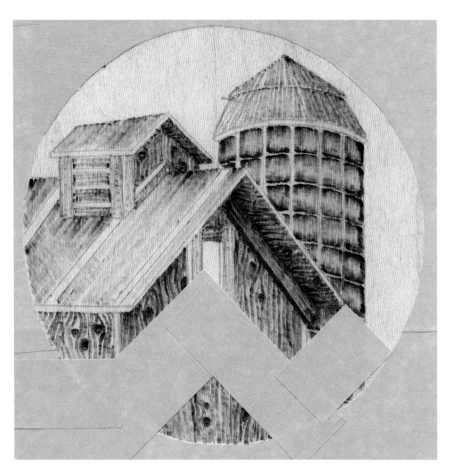

Mask the shadow lines. To make burning the shadows easier, cut and position painter's tape along the bottom edge of the large shadows on the main barn. This will allow you to pull your burning strokes from the edge of the rooflines in a clean, flowing movement over the tape. When you lift the tape, after the shading is complete, you will have a crisp, clean edge without the dark spot that often happens at the end of a stroke.

Deepen the shading tones. This photo shows the completed shading, after the mask of painter's tape has been removed. Work this entire step with the painter's tape in place to protect the lower areas of the barn wall from burning.

Use a flat spear shader or curved spear shader on a mid-medium temperature setting. Pull long, vertical line strokes from the edge line of the roofs to create the shadows under the roof overhangs. Fill these areas with an even coverage of coloring.

Shade the two far-right corrugated tin panels of the silo roof using a mid-medium temperature setting and flat spear shader. Shade the right wall and roof overhang of the cupola in the same manner.

Because the sunlight is at a low afternoon position, it does not cast a wide variety of shadow tones. Instead, the majority of the shadows in your scene will have an equal medium tonal value.

8 **Darken the silo and cupola.** Set your temperature slightly higher to a dark-medium value. Using the flat spear shader, darken the joint line of the cupola's roof overhang and right wall. Darken the framing board that trims the bottom edge of this wall.

Add a small, shallow line of shading to the silo and silo roof along the left side. Create a shadow line on the silo tiles under the tin roof.

With long, even line strokes, shade the right side of the silo wall. Remember to shade this same wall where it falls behind the right wall of the main barn.

On the main barn, darken the joint line between the right-side roof overhang and the trim board. Darken the lower edge of the trim board.

9 **Add fine details.** To begin detailing, first change to the ball tip or looped tip and to a temperature setting for a light-dark tonal value.

Fill in the right-side, main barn window and the gaps between the slates in the cupola wall with a solid black, touch-and-lift stroke.

Separate the main barn wall boards, the cupola wall boards, and the cupola roof boards with dark, solid lines to create individual boards. Vary these lines to add to the impression of age in the scene.

Detail the remaining small side boards, trim boards, and the boards in the overhangs.

Light touch-and-lift dots along the interlocking edges of the tin roofs give the impression of nails.

10 **Finish.** This barn scene is filled with texture—in the wall boards, the overhangs, the silo tiles, and the rusted tin roof. To keep the scene from becoming overpowered by detail, I chose to create my background trees in a dark-pale tone using a flat spear shader. The trees are made with a simple touch-and-lift stroke that burns a small triangle of color.

With a ball tip or looped tip and a light-dark to mid-dark temperature setting, burn a lightning rod on the top of the silo roof and two rods on the top of the cupola roof.

Remove the painter's tape mask that protected the wood surface outside of the circle of the scene. Erase any remaining tracing lines or guidelines with a white eraser. Remove the eraser dust with a clean, dry cloth. Apply two to three light coats of spray sealer.

Variation 4: Thatched Roof Barn

The previous three variations were worked using very linear building materials, such as sawn boards, square tiles, and tin panels. For this final variation, the materials used are much more organic in shape and in texture. Rounded field rock makes up the barn's side wall and hand-packed bricks are used to create the silo. Bricks, rocks, and thatching use fine- to medium-sized, sporadic dots to imply the texturing of the surface. So we will start this project by using a dot or scrubbie stroke pattern for the shading. The dot or scrubbie stroke shading can then be accented to become the texturing of the material that is used in each area of the design. Organic materials also have uneven, curved, or irregular edges, and the shadowing that we will work between the rocks and bricks is used to define those erratic edges. Since it takes more rocks or bricks to fill a barn wall than it takes to fill it using wood boards, the shadowing in this project becomes the dominant feature.

This barn treatment uses much more organic, irregularly shaped building materials.

SUPPLIES

- 9" x 10" (23 x 26cm) birch plywood
- Pen tips: ball tip and flat spear shader
- Polyurethane or acrylic spray sealer
- All basic board preparation supplies (see page 25)
- Pattern on page 162

ANALYSIS: SUNLIGHT

The light source for the Thatched Roof Barn comes from the upper left corner, at approximately 10 to 11 o'clock. This places the highlights on the roof of the main barn, the left side of the silo and silo roof, and along the left-side wall of the small attached structure on the silo.

ANALYSIS: SHADOWS

This mid-morning sun source shadows the right side of the main barn and deepens the value of the roof overhang. Note that this barn and silo do not have a cupola or mechanical venting system. Thatched roofs allow the steam from the drying hay and straw to escape naturally. Because small air channels are found throughout the roof, the entire roof allows for airflow.

PREPARING THE BOARD

1 **Sand.** Lightly sand the board using 220- or 320-grit sandpaper. Remove any sanding dust with a clean, dry cloth (more detailed instructions in Basic Board Preparation, page 25).

2 **Mark.** Mark the outer margins of the pattern area on the board using a pencil and ruler. The top and bottom margins are 1¾" (4.5cm) from the edge; the side margins are 1⅜" (3.5cm) from the edge. This centers the square area of the pattern on the board.

3 **Transfer.** Orient the board with the grain of the wood running vertically. Center the printed pattern on the board, tape it along the top edge to secure it, and transfer the design (more detailed instructions in Basic Board Preparation, page 25).

4 **Mask.** Cut four pieces of painter's tape. Lay the tape along the border of the traced design and lightly press into position.

BURNING THE BOARD

5 **Map the shadow areas.** Set your burning unit on a dark-pale temperature setting and using either a ball tip or looped tip to burn a tight scrubbie stroke into the main shadow areas. Use multiple layers of scrubbie strokes to create the deepest shadows under the main barn overhang, the small silo structure, and in the main barn window.

6 Add wood and stone textures.
Using a hotter setting for a mid-medium tone and a ball tip or looped tip, use the same tightly packed scrubbie stroke to work the shading along the bottom edges of the stones that create the main barn side walls.

Create the separations between the main barn boards in the upper story. Add some detailing to the ridge board under the roof overhang.

7 Shade the mortar. Turn your temperature setting up slightly to a dark-medium setting. With a ball tip or looped tip, fill in the mortar areas between the wall stones to a solid black-brown tone.

8 **Add thatched roof texture.** A touch-and-pull stroke creates a long, thin line with a dark point at the beginning. This is a perfect texture to create the thatching fibers of the roof. Turn your project upside down and work the touch-and-pull stroke so that each line is burned from the bottom edge of the roof toward the top of the roof. Allow these lines to curve and overlap to give the impression of long grass blades.

Detail the roof boards in the main barn overhang. Add a few knotholes in the upper-story wooden boards.

9 **Create handmade bricks in the silo.** The main structure of the silo is created with handmade bricks. Begin by burning the lines that represent the rows; allow these to have a slight curve that matches the curve of the bottom of the silo roof. Next, create individual bricks in each row with a vertical line. Alternate the bricks in each row so that one brick sits centered over the place that two bricks touch in the row below.

Detail the silo's tin roof by pulling long lines from the top of the roof toward the bottom edge of the roof. Use a touch-and-lift stroke along the bottom edge of the silo tin roof. These small, dark spots give the impression of the shadows cast by corrugated tin.

Add a lightning rod and rod stand to the top of the silo roof.

10 **Add background trees.** Move the temperature setting up to a light-dark setting. Add the thatching to the small structure on the silo with a ball tip and a touch-and-pull line stroke. Darken the silo structure window to black. Use the side edge of a flat spear shader to create the thin grain lines in the boards that make up the wall of the small silo structure.

Using a touch-and-lift stroke, create the pine tree background. Begin this work on a low temperature setting, create a few trees, and then increase the temperature to burn a few more on top of the work you just did.

11 **Finish.** Remove the painter's tape. Clean any remaining tracing or pencil lines with a white artist's eraser. Remove any eraser dust. Finish the scene with two to three light coats of spray acrylic or polyurethane sealer.

Creating an Atmosphere with Weather

The distant elements in your background can be used to establish the time of year, time of day, and even the weather conditions in which your landscape is set. Let's take a few moments and explore four samples of how you can create a sense of atmosphere. Prepare a blank practice board with four square areas and try to imitate the four atmospheric conditions shown here.

CLEAR SKIES AND SUNSHINE

If you burn your background elements with crisp, clean details, it implies a bright, sunny day. This trio of pines is all burned in a mid-range tonal value, where the trees become one cluster instead of individual trees.

On bright days, a field of grass like the one that lies beneath these pines will appear in a pale tonal value. Since each blade of grass reflects a tiny highlight of sunshine, that multitude of bright white spots gives the field an impression that it is a flat sheet of bright tonal values.

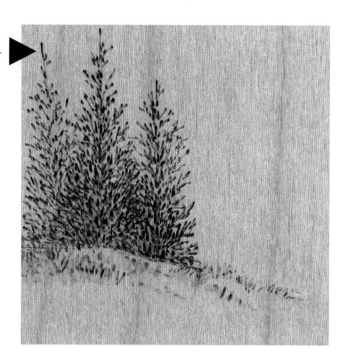

FOGGY MORNING

Air carries very fine particles of water. The more water in the air, the more foggy or cloudy your scene becomes. Because water-filled air is heavier than dry air, in the early morning the heavy, damp air appears as fog hanging close to the ground. The water droplets in the fog reflect the light in tiny highlights, giving fog a semi-transparent, white look.

In this sample, the morning fog obscures the lower portions of the pines. The white highlights of the grass blades on the ridge blend in with the white highlights of the fog, so you lose the defining line between the background air and the grass ridge.

SNOW

Snow clouds hold so much water that they take on a gray or mid-tone value coloring because the water content blocks the sunlight from passing thorough the cloud to your eyes. In this sample, that gray mid-tone hangs close to the ground where the water content is the highest.

Snow that falls or lies on pine branches or on the ground has a pale, even tonal value—usually white or slightly off-white. Snow is created by burning the areas or details around the snow clusters, allowing the clusters to remain at the original color of your media.

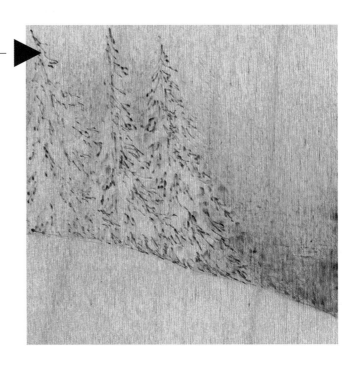

SUNSET AND IMPENDING STORMS

Both sunsets and impending storms diminish the amount of light available to the landscape. At sunset, the sun lies low against the horizon, bringing the sunlight into the scene at an almost horizontal angle. Since that light is behind any element in the scene, the side of the element that faces you is in full shadow. This same effect is found in impending thunderstorms, as the sky becomes dark along the horizon because of the tonal value depth of the storm clouds.

In this chapter, you will follow along in detail with four interesting burning projects that will each teach you about a new aspect of landscape burning. With each step in each project, you will be shown the tool to use as well as the temperature setting (based on the standard sepia scale from page 22). We'll cover a lot of ground—conceptually and geographically!—in this chapter, so get ready to learn a lot of skills and tips to apply to your future work.

After the Rain

FOCUS: CAPTURING WEATHER

After the Rain uses a heavily clouded sky, worked in mid-range tonal values, to create a rainy day atmosphere. The puddles in the roadbed that reflect portions of the barn and fence line show that you have captured the scene just moments after the storm has passed.

SUPPLIES
- 12" x 12" x ¼" (30 x 30 x 0.6cm) birch plywood
- Variable-temperature burning unit
- Pen tips: ball tip or looped tip, flat spear shader
- Craft knife or bench knife
- All basic board preparation supplies (see page 25)
- Pattern on page 163

1 **Prepare.** Prepare your board following the Basic Board Preparation instructions on page 25.

2 **Burn the background pines.** With either a ball tip or looped tip, on a mid-pale temperature setting, use short line strokes to create the cluster of pines on the left side of the scene. Work this step by turning your board so that you can pull each stroke from the ground level toward the sky.

Start with the cluster of pines at the left.

3 **Burn the mid-ground trees.** Raise your temperature setting slightly to a light-medium heat. Using a looped tip or ball tip, continue working the trees along the left-side horizon line of the pattern. Then repeat steps 2 and 3 for the trees just behind the barn on the right side of the design.

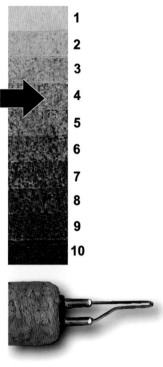

Continue adding trees.

4 **Work the fence posts and fence wire.** Because the fence line lies in the mid-ground area of the scene, the fence posts will show the shadows on either side of the round section of log, but will not show the detailing of the wood grain.

Use a ball tip or looped tip to shade along both outer edges of the posts to a medium tonal value. Add a paler value to the center of the posts. Work these shadings using a long pull stroke that runs vertically with the wood.

Add the fencing between each post by first drawing one long line of burning just below the tops of the posts for the full length of the fence. Work the bottom wire of the fence next, then add the center wire. Divide the remaining areas into one or two sections for your final horizontal fence wires. Add the vertical wires in the same manner. Defining the top, bottom, and center wires of any fencing will help you keep the wires evenly spaced.

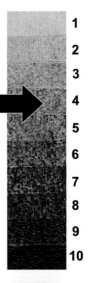

Next add the fence posts and delicate wires.

5 **Create the cloud bank.** Begin working your clouds on a mid-pale tonal value setting using a looped tip or ball tip. With short, curved line strokes, lightly define the tops of each individual cloud.

Change to a flat spear shader and, using the same temperature setting and short pull strokes, shade the lower section of each cloud where it sits behind another cloud. Add several layers of shading to the clouds until you have visually separate cloud areas. The darkest portion of the sky falls in the space between the mid-ground trees, right at the roadbed level.

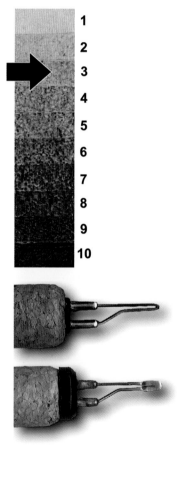

Form the clouds in the background.

6 **Darken the background trees.** Compare the tonal values of your background trees to the value of the clouds at the roadbed level. Darken a few of the background trees, if needed, to make them one or two tonal values darker than the clouds.

For my burning, I needed to intensify the trees about two tonal values to visually separate the trees from the low-lying clouds. This brought the reworked trees up to the darkness of my fence posts.

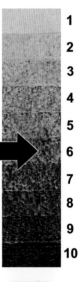

Deepen the tonal value of the trees.

7 **Add the grassy ridge and stone wall.** The looped tip or the edge of a flat spear shader creates very fine lines. On a cooler dark-pale temperature setting, pull long, curved lines for the grassy ridge just behind the stone wall on the right side of your design. Work the stroke by turning your board upside down so that you begin the stroke at the ground and pull the stroke toward the sky.

For the stone wall, detail the areas between the stones. This creates the shadow that separates each stone. Add some lighter tonal value shading to the stones in the lower half of the wall. The stones along the top of the wall are in sunlight and therefore do not have any shading.

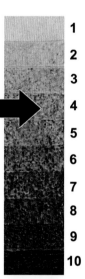

Move into the foreground with the stone wall.

8 **Start shading the barn walls.** The sky portion of this scene shows that the tops of the clouds do not reach as high in the scene as several of the background trees on the right side. This implies that the clouds are far enough away from our landscape that sunlight can reach the barn, tree, and road in the foreground.

Using a mid-medium temperature setting and a flat spear shader or curved spear shader, work the shadows beneath the roof overhang on the left side of the barn, on both outer sections of wall on the lower story of the left side, and on both right-side walls. Use long pull strokes to imply wood grain in your boards. Then add a second layer of shading near the overhangs on the walls to darken these shadows.

Using a flat spear shader and the same temperature setting, fill the underside of the overhangs to a solid medium-dark tone. Fill in the open door of the lower story of the barn. Add a few open holes in the board walls along the bottom edge.

Begin the barn.

9 **Shade the barn doors.** Setting your temperature into the darker value range of light-dark and, using a looped tip or ball tip, create solid black shadows along the trim boards in the upper story on either side of the hayloft door. Burn a black-toned line along the right side of the right-side barn door on the lower story and along the trim board at the corner of the front and side walls of the barn. Use a pencil to mark the vertical boards and bracing boards in all three doors.

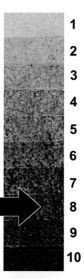

Work on the dark shadows of the barn doors.

10 **Establish the barn boards.** Lower the temperature setting to a mid-medium heat. Using a looped tip or ball tip, detail the barn wall boards with long, irregular lines that run vertically and by adding a few knotholes. Work a line of shading under the bracing boards on your doors. Also detail the barn doors.

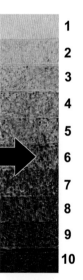

Add detail to the wooden barn boards.

11 **Detail the barn doors.** Add a few additional dark-toned lines in the detailing of your barn boards, especially in the shadows cast by the roof overhang.

12 **Start the puddle reflections.** Begin the work in the road puddles by copying the shading of the main scene in a tonal value that is one to two shades lighter than the reflected element. Because puddles are shallow, they usually show a tonal value that is slightly paler than the object they are reflecting. On the other hand, deep creeks, streams, or ponds will show a darker tonal value than the reflected element. This is because the depth of the water visually adds a layer of black beneath the reflection, giving the reflection the impression that it is darker.

Create the realistic puddle and reflection.

13 **Deepen the puddle reflections.** The lines in your reflections will not be either straight or long. Reflections often appear to be created with short, little spots of color and tonal value because of the rippling of the water. In this example, the shallow mud puddle is on a dirt road, and the natural ruts and ridges in the roadbed distort the reflection.

14 **Work the foreground tree.** Using a flat spear shader and a looped tip or ball tip, burn the foreground tree. Turn your piece upside down so that you can burn the tree lines from the main trunk toward the tips of the finest branches. The tree and branches are nearly solid black where they fall in front of the second story of the barn. The lower main trunk area of the tree is shaded along both outer edges to a black-dark tone, and the central area is filled with a medium tonal value.

Focus on the foreground tree.

15 **Cut bench knife highlights.** To complete the puddle reflections, set your temperature setting to a mid-medium. Using a flat spear shader or curved spear shader, drag several long, wide, horizontal lines across the puddle reflections. These lines should be slightly darker than the reflection work done in steps 13 and 14. They imply the top surface of the water. Then, using a craft knife or bench knife, cut several thin, horizontal V-gouges in your puddles. To make these cuts, first angle the blade slightly away from vertical to the wood and make the first cut. Then return to the beginning of the line, slightly slant your knife away from the line on the opposite side of the first cut, and pull the second cut. This will lift a thin strip of wood from your board, creating a bright white highlight that runs through the mid-tone burning of the puddle reflections.

Also add cut highlights to a few of your tree branches.

16 **Finish.** With your burning complete, erase any remaining tracing lines or guidelines with a white eraser. Remove the eraser dust with a clean, dry cloth. Apply two to three light coats of spray acrylic or polyurethane sealer.

Use a knife to cut strong highlights.

Climbing Tree

FOCUS: CREATING DEPTH THROUGH TONAL VALUES

While air has no color and does not reflect the sunlight, the moisture contained in the air does. The small water particles in the air reflect the light in a multitude of tiny, bright white highlights. The further back into a scene we look, the more white water-droplet highlights there are between us and the background elements. This makes objects appear paler the further back into the landscape they fall. In this piece, we will work through how to create a sense of distance in our landscapes through the use of graduated pale tones in the far background elements, which will contrast with the mid- and dark tones of the foreground.

SUPPLIES

- 12" x 12" x ¼" (30 x 30 x 0.6cm) birch plywood
- Variable-temperature burning unit
- Pen tips: ball tip or looped tip, flat spear shader
- Craft knife or bench knife
- All basic board preparation supplies (see page 25)
- Pattern on page 164

1 **Prepare.** Prepare your board following the Basic Board Preparation instructions on page 25.

2 **Start the far background tree line.** The most distant elements in the landscape are the two lines of trees behind the main barn complex. These will be the palest tonal values in the scene. Set your temperature setting on a mid-pale tonal value. Using a flat spear shader, create the tree lines using short line strokes. Work this step with your board upside down so that you are pulling the lines from the roofline of the barns toward the sky area. Your trees are darkest near the barn roof or ground line and become paler as they reach into the sky area.

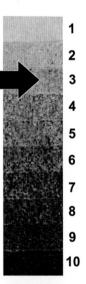

Start with the trees behind the structure.

3 **Work a second layer of background trees.** Using the same temperature setting and pen tip as you used in step 2, work a second layer of shading into the background trees along the bottom edge of the tree line.

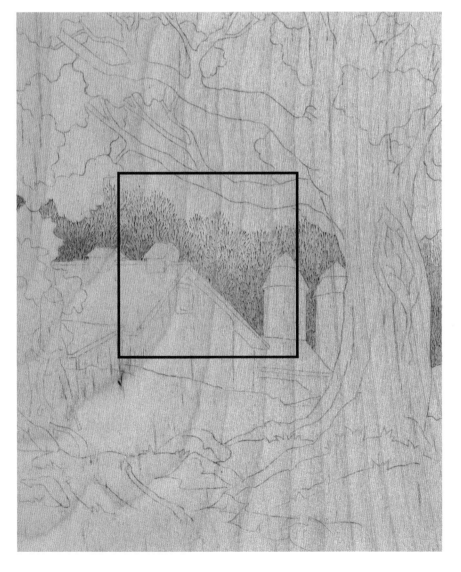

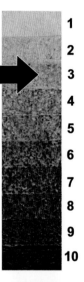

Enhance the trees.

4 **Create individual trees.** In this step, establish a few individual tree shapes in the foreground of the background trees. To keep these trees in the far distance, do not work any branches or trunks, which only appear in mid-ground and foreground trees. Instead, raise your temperature setting slightly to a dark-pale, then use a flat spear shader with a light pressure touch-and-lift stroke.

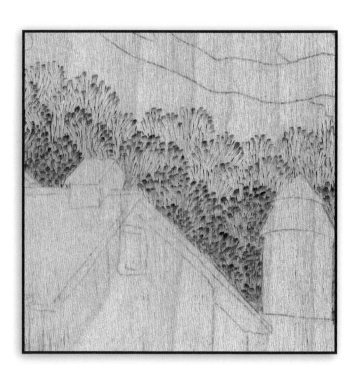

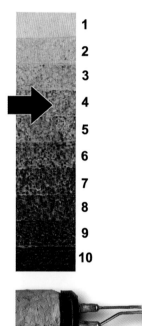

1
2
3
4
5
6
7
8
9
10

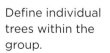

Define individual trees within the group.

5 **Burn a grass ridge in the mid-ground.** While your temperature is at a dark-pale setting, use a flat spear shader to establish the upper edge of the grass ridge in front of the barn complex. Use a light pressure touch-and-lift stroke.

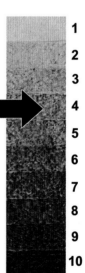

1
2
3
4
5
6
7
8
9
10

Move to the grass ridge in the mid-ground.

6 **Start shading the barn structures.** The flat spear shader can be used in a long line stroke to evenly shade your barn structures. This is a gentle touch-and-pull stroke. Work this step on a low temperature setting for a dark-pale tonal value. The sunlight source for this barn is coming in from the 1 to 2 o'clock position, which casts the shadows on the left-hand side of the structures.

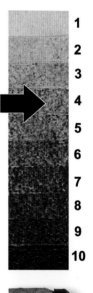

1
2
3
4
5
6
7
8
9
10

Work on the shading in the barn structures.

7 Deepen the shading on the barn structures.
Using the same temperature setting, stroke, and pen tip, darken the overhang areas of the main barn roof, cupolas, and small add-on barn structures. Because we are carefully controlling the graduation of pale tones in the background elements, working in light layers of burning allows you to slowly bring your shading up in tonal value without necessarily changing your temperature setting.

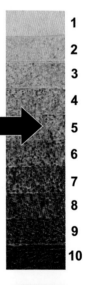

Enhance the shading in the barn structures.

8 **Detail the barn roof overhang.** Using the same temperature setting and pen tip, darken the shadows in and under the roof overhangs. Fill in the opening in the tractor shed and the windows to a medium tonal value. Using the edge of your flat spear shader, detail the roof boards and the trim board in the main barn overhang.

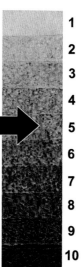

1
2
3
4
5
6
7
8
9
10

Add detail to the barn overhang.

9 **Create wall boards and roof shingles.** Using the same temperature setting and pen tip, create the wall boards using a long, straight pull stroke. Allow some areas of the barn walls to remain unburned to place some white boards between the medium tonal value boards.

Use short, straight line strokes to shade the top edges of the roof shingles. Short, straight lines are also used to burn the stones into the silo walls.

Changing to a looped tip or ball tip, add detailing lines along the barn structures. Darken the edges of the shingles along the roofs and add a roof ridge to both the main barn and cupola. Create corrugation lines in the tin roofs of the cupola and silo.

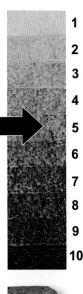

Add detail to the barn walls and roof.

10 **Add mid-ground leaf clusters.** The mid-ground leaf clusters in the large oak tree are created using a touch-and-lift stroke with a flat spear shader on a light-medium setting. Begin the leaf work with the clusters that fall behind the branches and trunk. The longer you allow the tip to touch the wood, the darker that stroke will become.

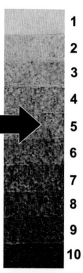

Start working on the leaves of the foreground tree.

11 **Darken the leaf clusters.** Repeat step 10, allowing your pen tip to remain for a little bit longer on the wood to create dark-toned leaves along the top and left edge of the pattern rectangle. Darken the leaves behind the tree trunk on the right side of the scene.

At this point in the project, you can see that the barn structure and tree lines worked in steps 2 through 9 have been visually pushed into the background by the darker tonal values of the leaf clusters.

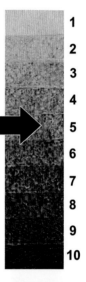

Darken the leaves.

12 **Shade the front edge of the grass.** Lower your temperature setting to a dark-pale. Using a flat spear shader, shade the front edge of the grass area where it touches the foreground path, post, and tree.

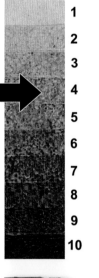

Start shading the grass.

13 **Shade the tree trunk and branches.** With a looped tip or ball tip and a light-dark temperature setting, shade the outer edges of the tree trunk. Use a scrubbie stroke for this step to imply tree bark. Shade along the fold and ridge lines inside of the tree trunk and work the hole in the right side of the trunk. Darken the branches that fall inside of the leaf cluster to a mid-dark tonal value.

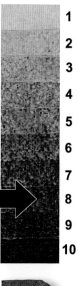

Add deep shading to the tree.

14 **Shade the center of the tree trunk.** Lower your temperature setting slightly to a mid-medium tonal value. Using a looped tip or ball tip and the scrubbie stroke, shade the center of the trunk with a lighter tonal value than the shading done in the previous step. Allow some unburned areas to remain in the central area and around the knothole to give a strong contrast to the dark-shaded edges.

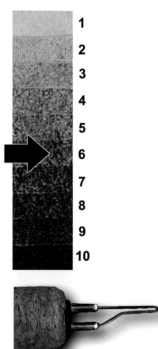

1
2
3
4
5
6
7
8
9
10

Work medium shading on the rest of the tree.

15 **Work the stones on the path.** The stones along the path are worked using a flat spear shader and long pull strokes. Work each stone with the pull strokes matching the angle of the stone's face. The high areas of the stones have the palest tones.

Add wood grain to the post with long, straight strokes. Allow the center area of the post to be paler than the edges.

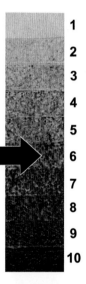

Create the stones on the ground.

16 **Shade the path.** Old, worn paths have two curved rut areas in the center of the walkway caused by the wear of wagon and tractor wheels. As you shade the path, use a mid-medium temperature setting and a flat spear shader. Start at the center ridge of the path and burn curved strokes that start low on the sides and are high at their center point. The two ruts, one on either side of the center ridge, are made with a reverse curve that is high on the edges and low at the center. Darken a few areas of the ruts to imply very deep cuts in the path.

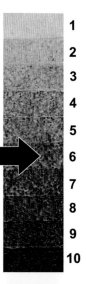

Shade the path and its deep ruts.

17 **Anchor the tree to the ground.** Using a light-dark tonal value temperature setting and a ball tip or looped tip, use long, curved lines to create the foreground grass. Turn your board upside down and pull the grass from the ground into the air space above it. The grass has the darkest tonal value in this landscape.

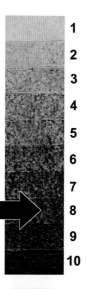

Add grass around the base of the tree.

18 **Add final detailing.** Using a light-dark temperature setting and a ball tip or looped tip, add some fine line detailing to the stones, path, and fence post. Detail the rope.

In the finished landscape, you will have a graduated tonal value, with the palest tones at the very back of the scene slowly developing into the darker tones in the foreground.

19 **Finish.** With your burning complete, erase any remaining tracing lines or guidelines with a white eraser. Remove the eraser dust with a clean, dry cloth. Apply two to three light coats of spray acrylic or polyurethane sealer.

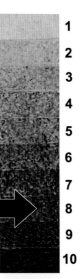

1
2
3
4
5
6
7
8
9
10

Add final details to the fence post, stones, and other areas.

Dark Stone Barn

FOCUS: CREATING DRAMATIC CONTRASTS

This project uses similar graduated tonal value shading to that used in Climbing Tree (page 79), with the palest tones in the far background to the darkest tones in the foreground, to create a personalized house sign. The dramatic contrast between the pale background and black tones in the foreground push the barn, fence, and trees forward in this scene.

SUPPLIES

- 12" x 12" x ¼" (30 x 30 x 0.6cm) birch plywood
- Variable-temperature burning unit
- Pen tips: ball tip or looped tip, flat spear shader
- Craft knife or bench knife
- All basic board preparation supplies (see page 25)
- Pattern on page 166

1 **Prepare.** Prepare your board following the Basic Board Preparation instructions on page 25. Then, measure 1" (2.5cm) from the edges of your plywood board. Using painter's tape or low-tack masking tape, tape along these drawn guidelines to protect the edges from your burning. Add one extra piece of painter's tape above the bottom strip. Using a pen and a small round object such as a bottle cap, mark a curved line at the lower two corners of the board. With a bench knife or craft knife, cut along the curves. Remove the tape on the inside area of the design. This will create a pleasing curved edge along the bottom of the design.

Use painter's tape and a knife to create a pleasing curve at the bottom of this piece.

2 **Burn the far background hills.** The work for this project begins in the far background with the burning of the three distant hills. Set your temperature to a dark-pale setting. Using a ball tip or looped tip and short, vertical lines, work the farthest hill first with lightly packed strokes. Work the middle hill in the same manner, adding more strokes to give it a slightly darker tonal value. Work the third hill, the one closest to the viewer, in the same manner, with a much denser packing of line strokes at the top of the hill. As you work down along this hill, reduce the number of line strokes to graduate the tonal value to the same value as the first hill. The number and density of the strokes changes the tonal value of the burn, despite the fact that the same pen tip and temperature setting are used.

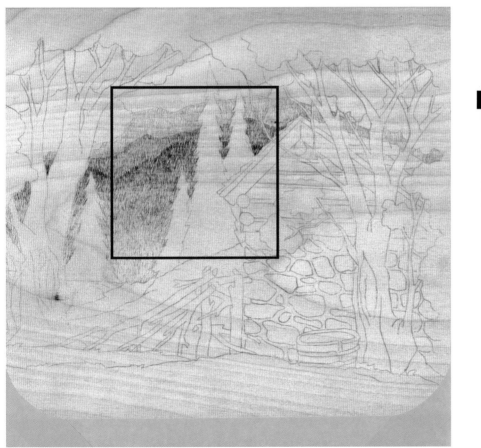

Start with the far background hills.

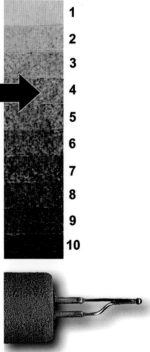

3 **Burn the mid-ground pines.** Increase your temperature setting slightly to a light-medium. Using a looped tip or ball tip and short, lightly curved lines, burn the tree pines in the background of the mid-ground area of the scene. Work these curved strokes from the lower outer side of each branch in upward strokes that are slightly angled toward the pine's trunk. Starting at the branch tip with this stroke makes the tips of the needle clusters darker than the rest of the curved line.

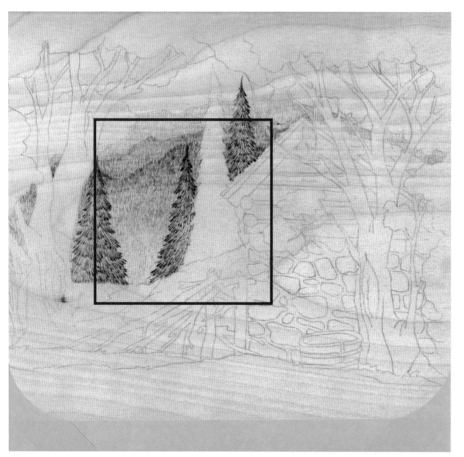

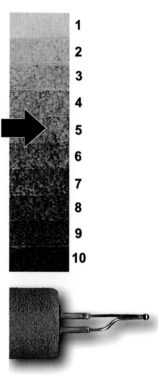

Move forward to start the mid-ground pines.

4 **Burn the large mid-ground pine.** Repeat step 3 for the large pine that stands in front of the previously worked pines. Use a denser packing of curved line strokes to make the tonal value of this pine darker than the other pines.

Change to a flat spear shader and create the black shadow on the left side of the pathway's grassy overhang using a curved line stroke. Add a few ruts and ridges in the path using the tip of the shader.

With a long, even pull stroke worked horizontally across the board, shade the grass area behind the twisted stick fence to a mid-pale tonal value.

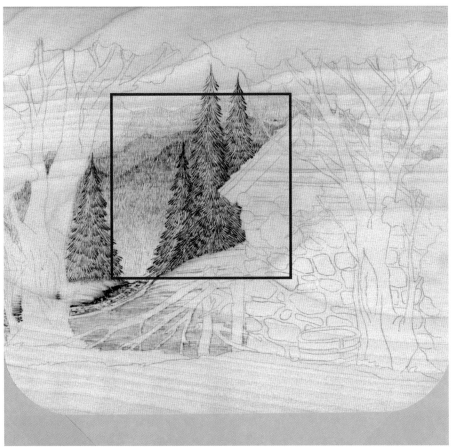

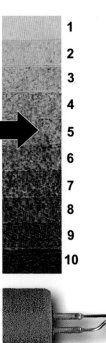

Finish with the largest mid-ground pine.

5 **Blacken the foreground leaf clusters.** Move into the foreground of your landscape to work the background cluster of leaves on the two foreground trees. Set your temperature to a light-dark tonal value. With a flat spear shader, use a touch-pause-lift stroke to burn a dark tonal value impression of the pen tip. Fill these clusters in tightly. These areas and the trees' trunks will become the darkest tonal value in the piece.

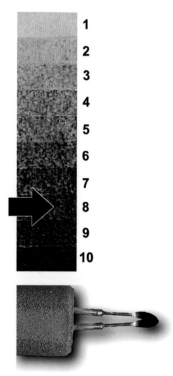

Make the foreground leaf clusters very dark.

6 **Fill in the personalization.** Personalization is easy when you use a word processing program on your computer. You can select the font style and size, and then print a copy that you can trace onto your design. With your personalization in place, use the same temperature setting and a ball tip or looped tip to fill in the name and house number to a solid black fill. Use a tightly packed touch-and-lift stroke.

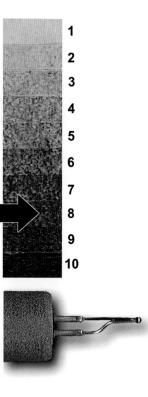

Work the personalized element of the piece.

7 **Add the mid-toned leaf clusters.** Work the next nearest clusters of foreground leaves using a flat spear shader and a mid-medium temperature setting. Tightly pack the touch-and-lift strokes to give an even coloring throughout these leaves.

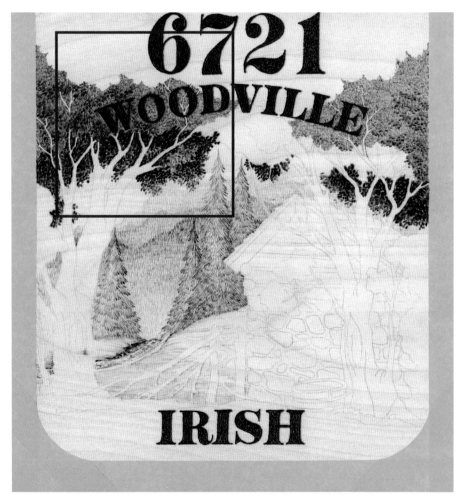

Start approaching the personalized element with medium leaf clusters.

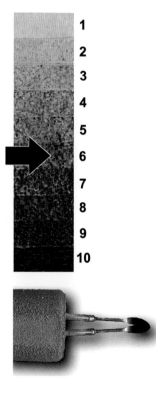

8 **Taper the leaves into the personalization.** As you near the personalized area of the design with your touch-and-lift strokes, begin making smaller and smaller isolated groups of leaves until ceasing to burn completely, leaving unburned wood near the top. In any landscape, you do not need to burn every detail—every leaf, every grass blade, or every board. You can create the element's main area and then taper off the number of burned strokes in the outer edges of the area back to white, unburned wood. In this burning, enough leaf clusters are burned to a dark tonal value to imply that the leaves of these trees continue above into the personalization area.

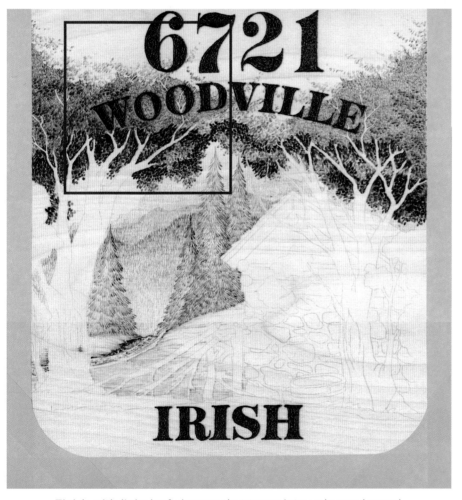

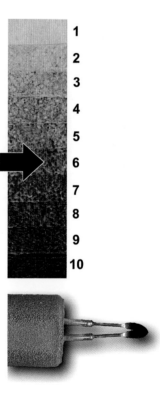

Finish with light leaf clusters that taper into unburned wood.

9 **Shade the left foreground tree.** Using either a looped tip or ball tip on a light-dark temperature setting, begin the dark shading on the right side of the left-hand tree. Use a tight scrubbie stroke to imply bark. You are working toward a very dark, almost solid tonal value.

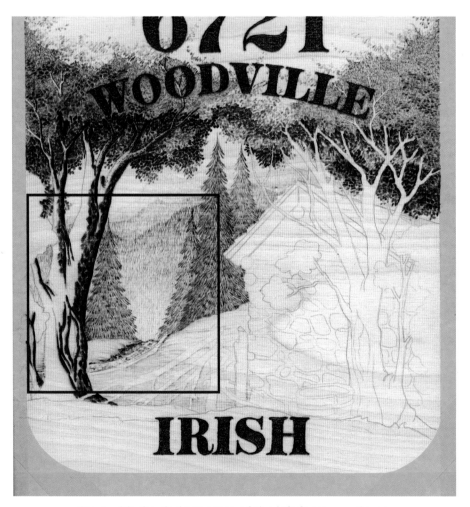

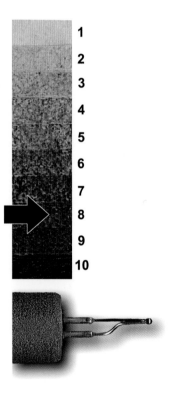

Start with the darkest areas of the left foreground tree.

10 **Finish the shading on the left foreground tree.** Using a flat spear shader and a light-dark temperature setting, fill in the remaining trunk and branch areas of your tree. Continue using the scrubbie stroke for a bark texture effect. The palest tonal value of the tree falls slightly off-center toward the left-hand side of the trunk. The darkest tonal value in the tree is found in the smallest tree branches inside the dark leaf clusters. The inside of the tree knothole should be almost solid black.

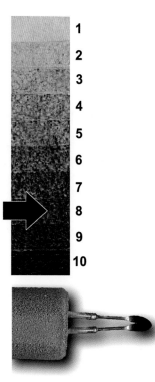

Complete the left foreground tree.

11 **Add the front leaf cluster.** The left-hand tree has several small clusters of leaves that fall in front of the tree trunk. Work these using a flat spear shader, a mid-medium temperature setting, and a touch-and-lift stroke. Work a few of the leaves directly over the work you did on the tree trunk.

12 **Establish the stone mortar.** Change to a looped tip or ball tip. Remaining on the mid-medium temperature setting, use a short line stroke or tight scrubbie stroke to burn the mortar areas between the stones in the barn wall and the shading between the boards in the roof area.

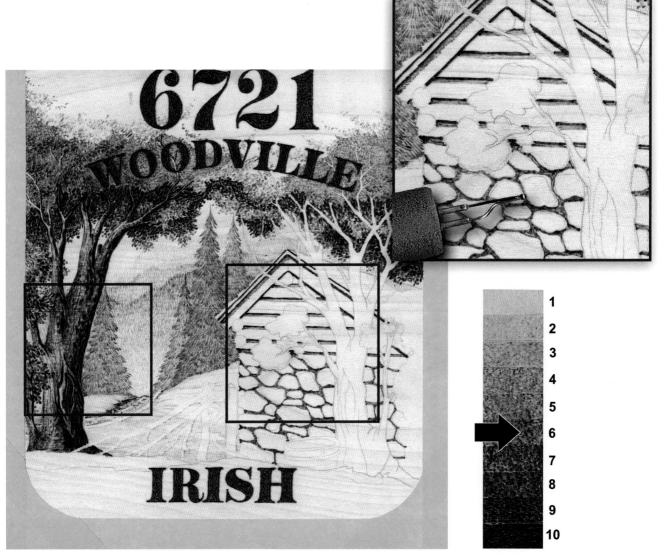

Start the stone mortar on the structure.

13 **Texture and shade the wall stones.** Using a ball tip or looped tip and a light-medium temperature setting, add horizontal grain lines to the boards in the upper story and roofline of your barn. Allow the lines to wave slightly to give the boards a hand-cut or hand-milled look.

Use a flat spear shader on the same temperature setting to shade the stones in the lower section of the barn wall. Work this step with a short touch-and-pull stroke. The stones in this wall are not perfectly cut, flat rocks. Instead, they have random high areas that are paler-toned than the dips and valleys, which may have a tonal value equal to the mortar work.

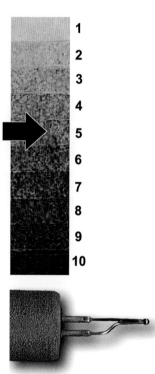

Add depth to the stones.

14 **Work the barn roof.** Using a looped tip or ball tip and a light-dark temperature setting, fill in the roof area of the barn with a solid touch-and-lift black tonal value.

At this point in the project, you should be able to see the dramatic contrast between the very pale tones of the background hills and the very black tonal values of the foreground trees, leaves, and barn roof. That contrast visually pushes the barn deeply under the tree canopy, shading it from any sunlight.

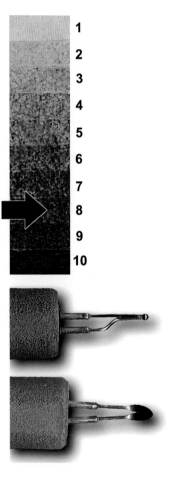

Burn the roof of the structure.

15 **Rework the upper story.** To darken the upper story of the barn, use a flat spear shader and a light-dark temperature setting. Use long, vertical pull strokes to evenly darken the entire wood area. Because you created the wood grain lines first in step 13 with a ball tip, you are now able to darken the wood areas of the barn without losing those grain lines.

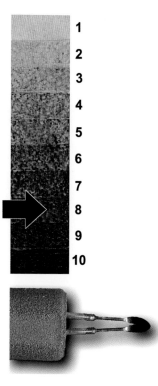

Continue darkening the roof of the structure.

16 **Add texture to the wall stones.** Add fine dots and crack lines to the wall stones using a ball tip or looped tip and a light-dark temperature setting. Darken all of the stonework, starting at the center of the wall and working toward the right-hand side of the barn. Deepen the shadow on the wall boards that fall below the roof ridge trim board. You can use a looped tip with a light pressure scrubbie stroke, or you can change to a flat spear shader for these shadow areas.

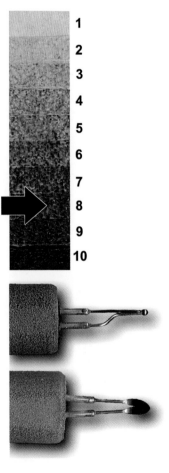

Add texture to the stones.

17 **Add the foreground right-hand tree and leaf clusters.** Set your temperature setting to light-dark. Use a looped tip or ball tip to fill in and texturize the tree trunk and branches on the right-hand foreground tree. You can use either a touch-and-lift stroke to create tightly packed dots or a short line stroke for the mid-toned central area of the tree.

Change to a flat spear shader to work the leaf clusters that lie in front of the right-hand tree and barn. Use a dark tone over the mid-toned boards of the barn. In contrast, use a mid-tone for the leaves that are in front of the roof.

18 **Burn the twisted stick fence.** Using a looped tip or ball tip on a mid-medium temperature, create wood grain lines in the branches and posts that make up the twisted stick fence. Add a second layer of lines for shading to the crossbar branches and the rear fence post.

Burn the remaining tree and the stick cluster.

19 **Burn the oak barrel.** Create and shade the oak barrel on the right side similar to how you burned the tree in step 17. The metal rim of the barrel is burned to a paler tone than the boards. With a looped tip or ball tip, pull a few long, curving lines from the barrel into the right side of the ground area to imply that the barrel is sitting on dirt, not grass.

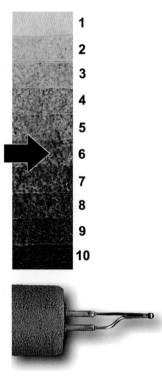

Create the shading and texture on the barrel.

20 **Burn the foreground grass.** Lower your temperature setting to a dark-pale tonal value. Using a flat spear shader and a long line scrubbie stroke, add just a touch of shading to the foreground dirt and grass areas. Use the edge of the shader and a touch-and-lift stroke to burn a line of grass blades along the bottom line of the left-hand tree, twisted stick fence, barrel, and right-hand tree.

21 **Finish.** With your burning complete, remove the painter's tape and erase any remaining tracing lines or guidelines with a white eraser. Remove the eraser dust with a clean, dry cloth. Apply two to three light coats of spray acrylic or polyurethane sealer.

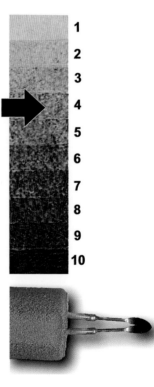

Wrap up with the foreground grass.

Barbed Wire Barn

FOCUS: ALTERING PATTERNS TO CREATE NEW DESIGNS

When I designed this pattern, I left the mid-ground fairly open, without the two fence lines, pines, tree line, or grass lines in the front field. These elements are easy to add to any pattern as you work your burning. During this project, we will explore the steps needed to alter any landscape pattern.

SUPPLIES
- 9" x 12" x ½" (23 x 30 x 1cm) basswood plaque
- Variable-temperature burning unit
- Pen tips: ball tip or looped tip, flat spear shader or curved spear shader
- All basic board preparation supplies (see page 25)
- Pattern on page 165

1 **Prepare.** Prepare your board following the Basic Board Preparation instructions on page 25.

2 **Burn the distant hills.** Using a flat spear shader or curved spear shader and a temperature setting for a dark-pale tonal value, begin this project in the far background hills. Touch the edge of the shader at the top edge of the hill and use a long pull stroke, worked on an angle, to create the ridges along the hillsides.

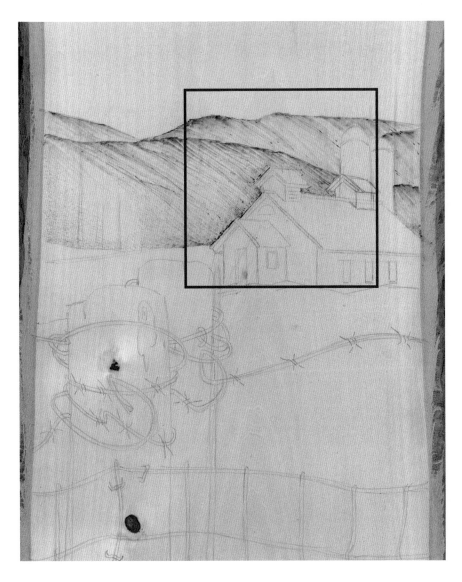

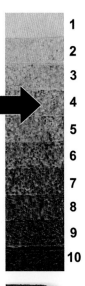

Start with the rolling hills in the far background.

3 **Create the background tree line.** Work the background tree line with a dark-pale temperature setting using a ball tip or looped tip. Use a touch-and-lift stroke to create the fine dots that make up this tree line. Create the cluster of three pines in front of the background tree line using the same temperature setting and pen tip. Let your tip stay on the wood for just a moment longer to allow these trees to have a slightly darker tonal value.

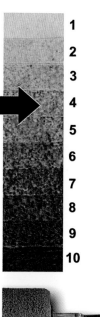

Create a line of trees in front of the hills.

4 **Burn the mid-ground grass fields.** Remaining on the dark-pale tonal value temperature setting, change your tip to a flat spear shader or curved spear shader. Use long pull strokes to create the ridges and furrows on the fields. Work the lines on an angle in the opposite direction to the lines of the hills. Add more lines where you want a darker shadow, such as where one hill lies behind another, where the field touches the base of the barn, and behind the front fence post.

Note that the field shading is worked around the foreground fence wire. This wire will be created by leaving it unburned and later adding just a touch of shading along the lower edge of the wire.

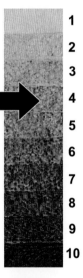

Move forward into the grassy fields.

5 **Add dark shading to the barn and silo.** Raise your temperature to a dark-medium setting. Using a flat spear shader or curved spear shader and long pull strokes, fill in the side walls of the barn, lean-to, cupolas, and silo. Start your pull strokes at the roofline of the structures and pull down toward the ground. This places the darkest point of the stroke in the shadow area of the roof.

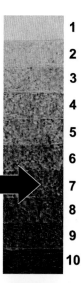

Add deep shading to the structures.

6 **Add mid-tone shading to the barn and silo.**
Lower the temperature for the flat spear shader or curved spear shader to a mid-pale setting. Repeat the long pull strokes from step 5 on the remaining sides of the barn, lean-to, cupolas, and silos. Also shade the roof overhangs with long pull strokes.

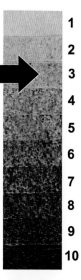

Add medium shading to the structures.

7 **Create corrugated roofs.** The impression of corrugated tin is created using a mid-pale temperature setting and a ball tip or looped tip. Allow a slightly wider strip of unburned white to remain between each of the corrugated lines you burn. With a ball tip or looped tip and the same temperature setting, create a line where the roof overhangs join the side of the structures.

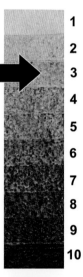

Draw lines in the roofs to create the effect of corrugated metal.

8 **Add detail to the barn.** Adjust your temperature to a mid-medium heat and, with a ball tip or looped tip, add detailing of barn boards, doors, windows, and the edges of the corrugated tin panels. Add vent lines and lightning rods to the cupolas. Burn the lightning rods on the silos. Lightly shade the windows and doors with a ball tip and a scrubbie stroke. Because the barn structure is in the mid-ground area of the scene, you do not need an abundance of details—just a little will be enough.

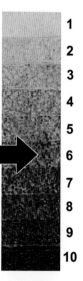

1
2
3
4
5
6
7
8
9
10

Add detail to the structures to give them realistic texture.

9 **Shape the fence posts.** Remain on the mid-medium temperature setting and, using a flat spear shader or curved spear shader, burn long pull strokes into the foreground fence post. Work your strokes around the fence wire. Burn the background post slightly darker than the foreground post by pulling the stroke slowly, leaving the pen tip on the wood for just a bit longer.

Change to a ball tip or looped tip and, using long line strokes, darken some of the grain lines in the posts, the shading in the cracks at the top of the post, and the small knotholes.

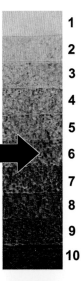

| 1 |
| 2 |
| 3 |
| 4 |
| 5 |
| 6 |
| 7 |
| 8 |
| 9 |
| 10 |

Work on the foreground fence posts.

10 **Add the small fence lines and detail the barbed wire.** With a flat spear shader or curved spear shader, create the small fence lines in the mid-ground of the scene. Use the flat side of the shader to draw in the fence posts. Use the sharp edge of the shader to burn very thin lines for the fence wire.

Detail the barbed wire on top of the fence wire. Use a tight S-shaped stroke to imply that the wire is several strands wrapped together.

Lightly pull a thin line, using the tip of your shader, along some areas of the bottom edges of the main fence wire. Do not completely outline the fence wire. This is a hit-and-miss stroke. Also add some detailing and shading to the fence staples.

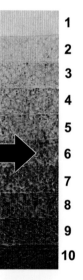

Add a new line of fence in the mid-ground.

11 **Add additional contrast.** Take a few moments to check that you have strong contrasts between each of your main elements—the hills, background tree line, barn complex, and foreground fence line. In my burning, I deepened the hill area behind the barn complex to strengthen the white tones in the barn roofs, and I also darkened the fence posts and some of the shading on the structures.

12 **Finish.** With your burning complete, erase any remaining tracing lines or guidelines with a white eraser. Remove the eraser dust with a clean, dry cloth. Apply two to three light coats of spray acrylic or polyurethane sealer.

Enhance the contrast in several elements of the piece, such as the fence post.

6

Capstone Project: Advertising Barn

This project, Advertising Barn, was first presented as an online forum post. It is now presented here in its entirety, with extra photos and instructions. We will divide the project into sections, analyze small details, and really dig deeply into all the thought and practice that can go into a complex, multilayered project—but you're going to learn so much from it. By the time you are done, you'll be ready to burn any challenging project you decide to tackle.

Advertising Barn

Before we dive into the burning itself, let's take a look at the six core features found in every element in a pattern, as well as some example of where these features can be seen in the Advertising Barn project. The six elements are: outline shape, texture, tonal value, contour, shadows and highlights, and detail.

Outline shape: *overall defined shapes and areas; for example, the rectangles that make up the walls of the barn.* Any element can be defined by its basic shape, as shown in the outline pattern of this design (see page 168). The side of the barn is created with one triangle on top of two stacked rectangles. You address the basic shapes of any design as you trace a pattern onto wood.

Texture: *details that create a physical, 3-D look; for example, the ridges created by the barn boards in the wall.* As the pen tip works across the surface of the board, it not only burns a tonal value, but also leaves an indent in the wood in the shape of the burned stroke. In this piece, the barn walls have a physical texture to them. Any texture created early on will remain throughout any other work that is laid upon it, so consider what texture stroke you will use in an area and what direction that stroke will take. For example, long, vertical lines create barn board texture, whereas half-circle curves create leaf cluster texture. Smooth, slick, or flat is also considered a texture.

Tonal value: *the placement on the sepia scale from light to dark; for example, the dark shadows in the car.* Each area has a base tonal value dependent on how it falls as a whole compared to the direct light source. The front barn wall in this piece has a lighter overall value than the side wall because the front wall receives more sunlight. The small leaf clusters at the bottom of the trees' branches have a darker tonal value because the light is blocked by the higher leaf clusters. The inner edge of the side wall roof, the overhang area, has a darker tonal value because it is totally blocked from the light.

Contour: *the curve or angles of an element or element area; for example, the rutted pathway.* Every area has contour, which can range from very flat to spherical. The curve of an element is created by graduated, deepening tonal values where the curve moves away from the light source.

Shadows and highlights: *how the sunlight is striking any area and what overhangs that area; for example, the highlights on the hood of the car.* Shadows and highlights are created by other elements in the pattern. The shadows in the side wall of the barn in this piece are created because the roof overhangs—that is, extends beyond—the wall, blocking the light. As a general rule of thumb, the contour and shadow of an element will be a darker tonal value than the shadow that it casts. So for this barn roof overhang, the overhang will be darker than the shadow it casts on the side wall. Highlights, on the other hand, are caused when a light source directly strikes an element or when light bounces off one element onto another. Not all highlights are pure white.

Detail: *the fine lines that define small lines or areas in an element; for example, the grill on the side of the car.* On top of everything lies the detailing—it is like the icing on a layer cake. Detailing is worked with regard to the general tonal value of the element. Dark elements will have darker tonal values, whereas pale elements will often have pale and mid-range values.

SUPPLIES

- 16" x 11½" x ½" (41 x 29 x 1cm) basswood plaque
- Variable-temperature burning unit
- Pen tips: ball tip or looped tip, flat spear shader, curved spear shader, square wire shader
- All basic board preparation supplies (see page 25)
- Pattern on page 168

Before beginning: Prepare your board following the Basic Board Preparation instructions on page 25.

Steps 1 through 12 focus on mapping the background landscapes areas, the trees behind the barn, and the barn walls. "Mapping" refers to the pyrography technique of establishing the tonal value relationships, shadowing, and light sources of each area relative to the surrounding areas, using a low temperature setting. For example, the barn walls in this piece are sectional with an upper board wall that overhangs the lower wall. By burning the walls first at a low temperature setting, you can create the vertical board textures, establish which wall is in sunlight and which is in shadow, and add a small area of shadowing on the lower wall at the overhang point. Later, as the burning develops toward completion, all of this early mapping work will be reworked to deepen the tonal values and add detail lines.

1 Beginning in the large tree leaf clusters to the left of the barn, use the curved spear shader on a light-pale temperature setting in a tightly packed curved stroke to establish the lower shading in the clusters.

2 Repeat step 1 in the same tree, working over the first layer of burning. This will darken the first shading and add pale shading to the tops of the leaf clusters. Also work this tightly packed curved stroke in the trees on the right side of the barn.

3 Using the side of the curved spear shader, shade the tree trunks using a light-pale temperature setting. Use a long pull stroke, starting at the top of the branch and working toward the bottom, or root area, of the tree.

4 As I began working the background grass ridge on the right side of the barn, I decided to add a small grass ridge behind the tree trunks on the left. This balances the background air space by including the same texture and tonal value burns on both sides of the barn. I drew in the new ridge with a pencil.

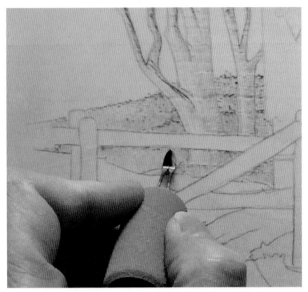

5 Using the flat spear shader and a light-pale temperature setting, work the background grass ridges in a short vertical pull stroke that creates small, individual grass lines. This stroke starts at the top of the grass ridge and pulls down toward the bottom of the piece.

6 Turn the board upside down to work the pine tree behind the barn. Using a light-pale temperature setting and the flat spear shader, fill the pine with long pull strokes. A slight hesitation will make the tip burn a little darker than the burn in the pulled portion of this stroke, which is what we want.

7 Using a mid-pale temperature setting, with the belly of the flat spear shader flat to the board, work a light layer of general, overall shading to all of the areas worked: the left and right side tree leaf clusters, the left side tree trunks, the grassy ridges, and the pine tree. Rubbing the back of this shader in small, tight circles gives a very even, overall shading.

8 You can lead the shader along a side edge by slightly tipping the pen tip. Do this to create a crisp but pale-toned line where the trees meet the sides and roof of the barn.

9 Keeping the flat spear shader with a mid-pale temperature setting, start to work the right side wall of the barn using a long pull stroke.

10 Work the barn board lines in two layers: one worked from the roofline toward the ground and the other from the ground back toward the roof. The side of this shader gives an even width to each burned line, which makes the texture for the barn boards uniform.

11 Before doing any shading work in the left side wall, I wanted to add the advertising lettering. This text is worked using the medium ball tip and a mid-medium temperature setting. This temperature setting is high enough to give a strong, dark lettering line, but not so hot as to cause haloing. Haloing is when the pen tip is so hot that it burns a black line where the tip touches the wood but also burns a paler-toned ring around the tip point. You end up with a black line haloed by a medium ring of burn, which is usually not what you want.

12 Using the flat spear shader and a light-pale temperature setting, work the board texturing into the left side wall of the barn. Work this step once from the roofline down, and then turn your board upside down to work from the ground up. The left barn wall is paler in value than the right side wall.

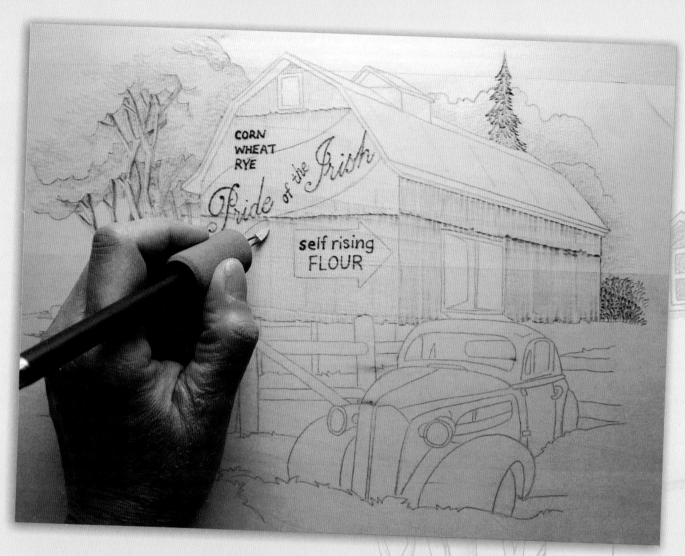

FOCUS: Planning Ahead for Tonal Value Differences

As I work any burning, I begin with a very pale value, then reburn the area as needed to slowly create layers of burnings that make up my finished tonal value. As we continue this project, you will see me return to one area over and over again.

Every area of a pattern—whether you are carving, burning, or painting—affects and changes the other areas of your design. In addition, the earliest tonal values that you use in a burning directly determine the tonal values you will have to use later to establish depth and contour.

As an example, based on where we are in this project, the tonal value of the barn determines the tonal value of the old car. To create enough contrast between the two, one must be a pale or medium tone and the other a dark or black tone. They cannot both be pale or medium or dark and still be distinguishable from each other.

The darker I burn the barn at this point, then, the blacker I will have to burn the car later. So, during these early burn layers, I do want some contrast between my background elements, but I want those tonal value changes to be small.

During steps 13 through 20, we will move the burning into the mid-ground area of the pattern, which includes the grass in front of the barn and the fence line. We will also start the darkest areas of the pattern, which are worked to set the deepest tonal range of the design. The dark areas include the lettering on the wall advertising, the windows and open spaces of the barn doors, the inside of the car, and the car's headlights and tires. Note that even though these areas will become the darkest tones, at this stage of the work the sepia value still remains in a mid-dark range of chocolate brown.

13 Using a mid-pale temperature setting and the flat spear shader, slightly darken the tonal value of the front grassy ridge under the fence line. This will create just a bit more contrast with the tree trunks and background ridges. This toning is done with the shader flat against the wood and with a tight circular motion.

14 Work the boards of the walls of the cupola in a long pull stroke using the flat spear shader and a mid-pale temperature setting.

15 Using the flat spear shader on its side edge and a mid-pale temperature setting, add some staggered, long pull shading strokes to the tin roof areas. Allow the shader edge to rest occasionally to create some darker, rusted areas in the tin.

16 Using the flat spear shader and a mid-pale temperature setting, create the barn boards in the doors with long pull strokes.

17 Using a dark-medium temperature setting, start to fill in the areas that will eventually become the darkest values in the pattern, using tightly packed touch-and-lift spots.

18 The darkest areas in the background include the barn loft window, the opening between the doors, and the lower-level door opening. The darkest areas in the foreground include the interior windows of the car, the wheel hub, and the headlights.

19 Using a dark-pale temperature setting and the side edge of the curved spear shader, shade the right side or underside of each fence post using a long pull stroke.

20 With the fence posts established, fill in the lower level of the barn with small touch strokes using the flat spear shader at a dark-pale temperature setting. Allow a small line of white to remain between each rock of this wall to create the feeling of mortar.

In these next steps, the background and mid-ground areas will be developed into deeper tonal values. The roof overhang will be shaded into the deep black tones and the shadow that it casts onto the barn wall will be worked. The boards that make up the side wall of the barn will be textured and separated into individual boards. At the same time, the double door on the side wall will be created. Work will also begin on the tin panels on the roof and the cupola.

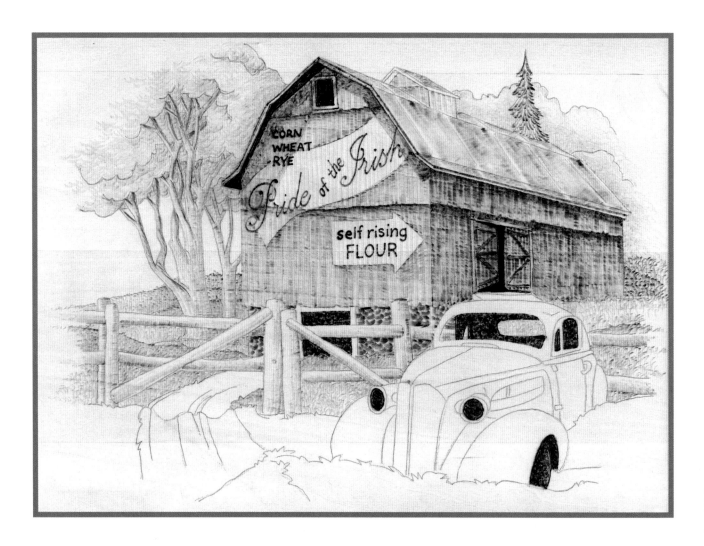

21 I decided that my right-side barn wall could go a touch deeper in value, so I worked a new layer of burning using long pull strokes with the flat spear shader and a light-medium temperature setting.

22 Shadows lie over the top of the contour and texture of an element. For example, if an apple is casting a shadow on an orange, that shadow falls on top of the orange's peel texture and spherical shape. We have already created the texture of the barn boards on top of the flat walls. The shadows can now be burned to fall on top of those features. Using the curved spear shader at a dark-pale temperature setting, add a shadow under the top level of side wall boards on the right side of the barn. This is a long pull stroke that runs horizontally under that board ridge. Work a shadow in the same manner under the roofline along the side wall.

23 Using the flat spear shader and a mid-medium temperature setting, fill in the door support boards. Use the edge of the shader to create long, clean lines.

24 To bring the doors up to the same tonal value as the right side wall, use the flat spear shader at a light-medium temperature setting with long pull strokes. The door that is set inside of the barn is slightly darker in value than the door that is level with the barn wall.

25 To straighten and strengthen the barn door lines, use the ball tip at a mid-medium temperature setting.

26 At a dark-pale temperature setting, using the curved spear shader, add a few areas of darker board lines to give a little more variety along the right side wall.

27 To deepen the left barn wall and create the impression of the painted advertisement, burn a second layer of long pull strokes in all of the barn boards except the area inside of the ad banners. Use a dark-pale temperature setting and the flat spear shader. To give a small amount of difference in the large curved banner that is in the lower wall section, burn the boards using a mid-pale temperature setting—just enough to make this area a little darker than the banner area in the upper wall section.

28 The shadowing of the wall overhangs is worked just as was done in the right side wall, using a dark-pale temperature setting and pulling the flat spear shader in a long horizontal line under each overhang.

29 The outer left-side edge of the roof extends beyond the side of the barn wall; this roof overhang casts a deep shadow onto the wall. Using a ruler and pencil, mark shadow guidelines to follow.

30 Since the light source (in this case, the sun) is in the upper left corner, the right side of the barn roof also shadows the wall, but with a narrower shadow area. Mark this line using a ruler and pencil.

31 Laying the flat spear shader flat to the board on a mid-medium temperature setting, use tight circular strokes to create the roof-cast shadows. Work right over the advertising banner areas—they will naturally come out a lighter value than the surrounding barn boards.

32 Next we will deepen this area of shadowing. In order to avoid creating a dark, crisp line at the inner edge of the shadow, erase the pencil lines first. This will prevent you from accidentally setting those pencil lines with the tip.

33 The closer to the roof overhang an area of the wall is, the darker the shadow it will hold. Because of this, rework the shadows along the wall near the roofline using the flat spear shader, a dark-medium temperature setting, and a long pull stroke that follows the direction of the roofline.

34 For the black tones of the roof overhang itself, use the ball tip and a dark-medium temperature setting. This is the hottest setting you have used so far in this project. A tightly packed touch-and-lift dot stroke or tightly packed scrubbie stroke brings this area to an even mid-dark tone. Also darken the hayloft window, where the shadow crosses the opening, with the ball tip. Note that the small, lower right-hand-side triangle of the opening is allowed to remain at its original dark-medium toning.

35 With the ball tip in hand, establish the outer line of the barn wall and the rooflines with a simple, straight line worked at a mid-medium temperature setting.

36 To darken the edge of the side wall overhang and create the feeling of uneven board ends, use the flat spear shader and a dark-medium temperature setting in a touch-and-lift stroke to burn a few dark V-shaped areas.

FOCUS: Telling a Story with Your Pyrography

When you work any landscape scene, you are telling a visual story that goes beyond shadows, highlights, and details. Think about where your landscape is located in time and geographic space. For example, in this piece, the small structure on the top of a hay barn is called a cupola, and cupolas are often found in the mid-Atlantic region of the U.S. These delightful little additions in older barns are often ornate in structure. They are venting systems that allow the heat and steam that build up from freshly cut, baled, and stored hay to escape. Without cupolas, the barns in the mid-Atlantic can literally burst into flames during the hot, humid summer months. On top of the cupolas or running down the roof ridge, mid-Atlantic barns also always have a series of lightning rods, which help ground a lightning strike and hopefully prevent the barn from turning into a deep pile of ashes. These are just a few small examples of how knowing the story of your landscape can help you add authentic and interesting details.

By beginning this project with a low-temperature mapping and slowly developing each area of the work with new layers of burning, you have total control over the tonal value changes of a design. During the coming steps, many of the areas in the background and mid-ground will receive their last layer of burning to establish defined pale, medium, dark, and black tones throughout the scene. Detail lines and accent lines will be added to the barn boards, roofline, fence, and roadbed. During this phase, we will also see how easy it is to correct a mistake by sanding or carving the wood.

37 In the previous step, you can see an extra dark spot at the top of the right-side wall door—a mistake caused by hesitating for just a moment too long with the pen tip on the wood. If you accidentally create a similar error on your piece, remove the area by using the tip of a fine grit foam core fingernail emery board. By lightly working the board over the excess burn area, you can remove just enough of the black tone to take out the spot without losing all of the tonal value work in that area. Mistakes can also be lifted or cut away using a craft knife or woodcarving gouge.

38 Using the flat spear shader at a mid-medium temperature setting, add a slightly darker value to that inner door to clearly position it as sitting inside the barn.

39 To darken the foundation of the barn, work with the flat spear shader at a mid-medium temperature setting.

40 To add a few dark shaded lines in the tin roof, use the edge of the flat spear shader at a dark-pale temperature setting, and a pull stroke. These lines are being worked so that there are a few breaks in some of the lines and some are slightly darker than others, but all run in the direction of the tin panels.

41 Add shading to the roof overhang on the cupola, the shadow cast by this roof overhang on the cupola sides, and few vent lines in the front cupola wall, plus a screen wire mesh line pattern on the side wall of the cupola. Use the flat spear shader on a dark-pale temperature setting for these details.

42 At a dark-pale temperature setting using the flat spear shader, create a cast shadow from the cupola onto the tin roof. Darken the side wall of the cupola to be just slightly darker than the cast shadow tones.

43 Work fine detailing lines into all of the barn wall boards using the curved spear shader at a mid-medium temperature setting.

44 Strengthen the V-shaped rotted board edges using the point of the curved spear shader and a mid-medium temperature setting.

45 Moving into the roof area, use the ball tip at a mid-pale temperature setting to establish the long, slanted lines that define the tin roof panels.

46 Roofing panels are often corrugated. To create the ripple effect of the corrugated edging, use the ball tip on a dark-pale temperature setting to mark a series of five to six small dots along the roof edge. A second line of dots falls on the angle of the center, large roof area, and a third row falls at the bottom of the top roof area. To create the staggered or stepped effect of corrugated panels, create three alternating rows of dots, referring to the photo for placement.

47 Lightning rods can be added to the roof ridge and to the rooftop of the cupola using a ball tip on a dark-pale temperature setting.

48 Moving back to the foundation wall on the front of the barn, add a few dark tonal value lines between the stones using a ball tip on a mid-medium temperature setting.

49 To add more contrast in the foliage, use the flat spear shader on the flat at a mid-pale temperature setting to deepen the underside areas and background areas of the foliage.

50 Deepen the shading in the tree trunks and branches using the flat spear shader at a mid-pale temperature setting. First use it on the flat for the middle and right side shading, then on the edge along the right side outlining.

51 At this point, the background work is complete enough to move into the foreground areas—the fence line, roadbed, and old car.

52 The dividing line of the foreground and mid-ground/background in this pattern falls along the fence line. The posts and boards of the fence are foreground, but the fence also captures areas of the background within its openings. To reinforce the grass areas captured inside that fence, work a few outline areas at the top of the background grass ridges using the ball tip and a mid-pale temperature setting.

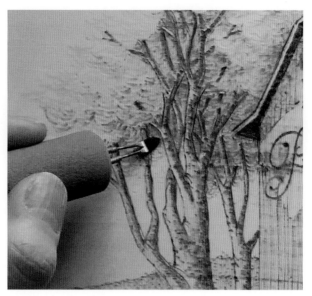

53 As you reinforce those areas, also establish the left side of the tree branches by using the tip of the flat spear shader at a mid-pale temperature setting.

54 During the steps that worked the grass ridge in front of the foundation wall, in my burning I lost the top portion of the roadbed. By placing the ruler on the roadbed at the fence posts in the foreground and on the lower right-hand corner of the open door in the foundation wall, I marked a pencil line where the roadbed should lie.

55 Using the flat spear shader at a dark-pale temperature setting, a scrubbie stroke cancels out the earlier grass lines and tones in this road area.

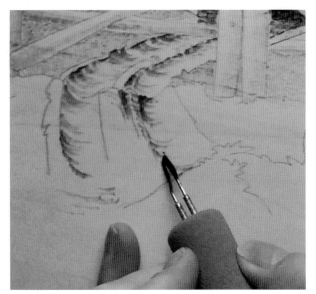

56 Use the curved spear shader at a dark-pale temperature setting to create the ruts in the foreground roadbed. Hold the side of the curved spear shader against the right-side edge of the roadbed lines. A pull stroke creates a nice comma-shaped, graduated burn.

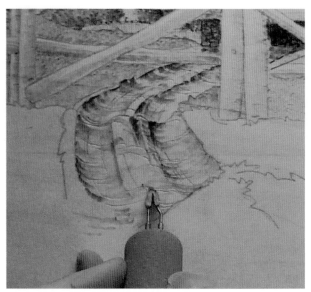

57 This photo gives an overview of the roadbed comma strokes that imply ruts and ridges in the dirt.

58 Return to the flat spear shader. With the particular brand and tips I am using here, this tool's tip is more blunt than the crisp, sharp edge of the curved spear shader. Therefore the curved spear shader would cut an extremely thin line, whereas the shader will lay a slightly wider line on the wood. At a dark-pale temperature setting, working the shader on its tip, add more ridge and rut lines in the roadbed area.

59 At this point in my work, I needed to make a second pattern correction, as I also lost the fence rail that should have been visible through the back window of the car. I aligned the ruler to that rail on both sides of the car and then marked the line inside of the window using a pencil. Using the curved spear shader and a mid-pale temperature setting, I burned the window fence rail in long lines to match the other fence lines.

It's time to move into the foreground of the design by working the roadbed, front grass ridges, and the old car. To make the car become the focal point of the pattern, we will use two simple techniques: dramatic tonal value change and a stand-alone texture pattern.

Placing one large area of extremely pale tonal value against a large area of your blackest tonal value, you draw the eye to the area where they touch. In this old car, the left side of the roof and hood are in full sunlight, the palest tonal value of the burning. The inside of the car, headlights, and tires are all trapped in shadow and are the darkest values of the work. Dramatic contrast creates attention, so the sudden change from white to black pulls the eye right to the car.

The second technique we will use is texture. Throughout the barn and landscape areas, we have used line work: long lines in the barn boards, short, wide lines in the roof, and short, curved lines in the grass and trees. For the car, we will use a new texture: a tightly packed scrubbie stroke worked with the flat spear shader. This is the only place in the project that uses this texture, bringing that area extra attention.

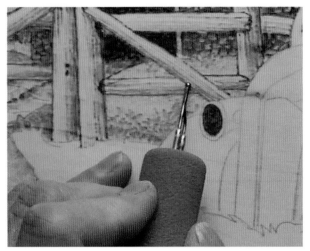

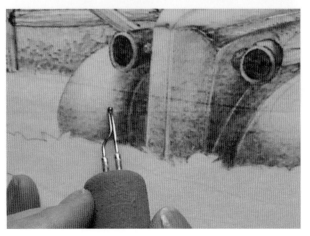

60 Since the top edges of the fence rails have no burning—they are still the white tone of the unburned wood—we need to establish those edges of the rail. Using the ball tip on a dark-pale temperature setting, burn a light-medium long line across the rails. Add that same light-medium line on the other posts and rails wherever the fence seems incomplete.

61 The work on the car begins with mapping the contour shading using the flat spear shader on a dark-pale temperature setting. For this shading, use the shader on the flat in a circular or scrubbie stroke. The contour shading for the old car falls on the right-hand side of the roof, along the right-side edge of the hood, and in the right side and door. The side of the hood area on the right side is as dark in value as the car's side and door.

62 Continue mapping using the same tip, temperature setting, and stroke pattern on the left side of the car. Both front fenders are half spheres with the cut half of the sphere laid in the foreground grass. This puts the contour shading on the right sides of the fenders and where the fenders met the grass. Contour shade the headlights.

63 Develop the tonal value shading in the old car to bring the areas above the wheel fenders into a dark-medium tonal value. In this image, you can see that I have marked in pencil an oval on the top of the right-hand front fender. This oval marks an area that I will not be burning. I want to keep this area the palest tonal value of the unburned wood. The other areas in this old car that will remain unburned (and that you may wish to mark) are the top of the left fender, the left side of the front grill, the left side of the hood, the left side of the roof, and the metal area in the front of the car that surrounds the front window glass.

64 To give this car a rusted appearance, change to the ball tip on a dark-pale temperature setting and use a tight, circular scrubbie stroke. Rework all of the shading done in the previous two steps to darken those areas. Also begin to work some shading radiating out from those areas. Then turn the temperature setting up to mid-medium and rework the darkest value areas in the contour shading along the right side of the car, the right side of the hood area, and the front fenders. Also add shading along the ridge down the center of the hood: on the right side, the lines that mark the door opening, the lines that mark the side vents, and along the lines that mark the window rubber. Add line work to the vents and in the detail lines between the hood side and fenders.

65 The car will naturally cast a shadow on the ground on the right side. Use the flat spear shader on the flat at a dark-pale temperature setting in tight, circular shading strokes to tone the grass.

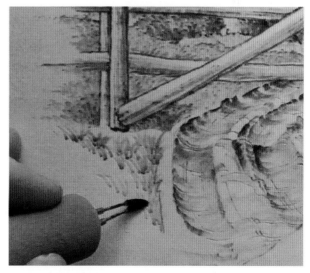

66 A little darkening is needed in the grass ridge area captured inside of the fence line. Use the curved spear shader at a light-medium temperature setting to burn this.

67 Also work some shader strokes in the grass ridges in front of the car and in the grass ridge to the right of the roadbed.

68 Using the side of the curved spear shader on a dark-pale temperature setting, work an even pull stroke layering of toning over all of the background elements that come into contact with the car. Work this shading from the intersection with the car to about 1" (2.5cm) into the surrounding areas, with the darkest areas of shading adjacent to the car.

69 Work the same toning as worked in the previous step on both sides of the car area, including over the fence posts and in the open side and back window areas of the car. Also shade the side barn wall and ramp here.

70 Next, use the side or edge of a flat spear shader or the point of a curved spear shader to burn the individual tall, dark grasses in the foreground of the scene. However, if you have the Optima I set that I used here, try to use the specialty tip that I used instead: the coarse hair tip, unique to the Optima I, is the perfect choice for this grass. This tip cuts a wide V-shaped trough as it burns, and the V-edge of the tip burns a hot line. I turned my project upside down so that I could put the point of the tip at the ground point of the grass blade then pull the tip through the stroke. Work the individual grass lines over the car. Dark grass lines surround the car at ground level along the car's right side and in front of the car. The front line of grass extends to the edge of the front roadbed. The grass lines I created here with the coarse hair tip are far stronger than any other detailing line worked so far with any of the other pen tips.

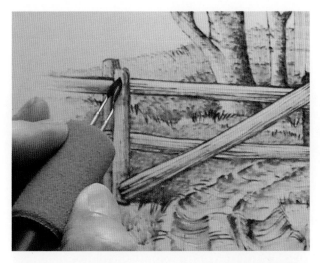

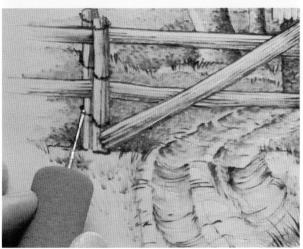

71 Using the curved spear shader at a mid-medium temperature setting, add a fair amount of fine line detailing throughout the entire scene. In the barn, add fine, long lines between the boards, some outlining around the hayloft window, and some detailing around the outer edges of the doors. Along the right-side edges of the tree trunks and branches, add a few short detail lines, especially where a branch joins the main trunk. A line of short, curved strokes along the tops of the background grass ridge helps to separate one ridge from another. In the foreground area, add to the fence posts and rails, mostly in the shaded areas.

72 With a mid-medium temperature setting and the ball tip, close the old gate by adding a rope tie over the right-side gateposts and two rope hinges on the left side.

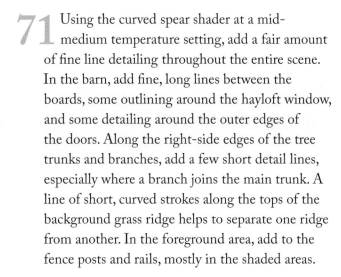

73 After you have closed the gate, it's time to get a pencil and lightly write or print your name and the year in the lower right-hand corner of the piece, just under the front right fender. Using the ball tip and a mid-pale temperature setting, sign and date your work.

74 Clean any remaining tracing or pencil lines with a white artist's eraser. Remove any eraser dust. Finish the scene with two to three light coats of spray acrylic or polyurethane sealer.

7 | Patterns and Inspiration

In this section you will find all of the patterns used and referenced in this book, plus a whole host of additional patterns for you to try out, practice with, and customize to your own needs. Most patterns come accompanied by either a shading guide (the pattern shaded with pencil) or a burned pyrography sample. You can reference these guides and samples as you burn your own work, or you can ignore them and follow your own instincts. Photocopy any pattern you want to use at the size appropriate for the project you want to make.

Quilt Barn Texture Practice Board pattern
© LORA S. IRISH

Quilt Barn Texture Practice Board pyrography
© LORA S. IRISH

Patterns and Inspiration **157**

Basic Roof Barn pattern
© LORA S. IRISH

Wood Board Roof Barn pattern
© LORA S. IRISH

Cedar Shingles Roof Barn pattern
© LORA S. IRISH

Tin Roof Barn pattern
© LORA S. IRISH

Thatched Roof Barn pattern
© LORA S. IRISH

After the Rain pattern
© LORA S. IRISH

Climbing Tree pattern
© LORA S. IRISH

Barbed Wire Barn pattern
© LORA S. IRISH

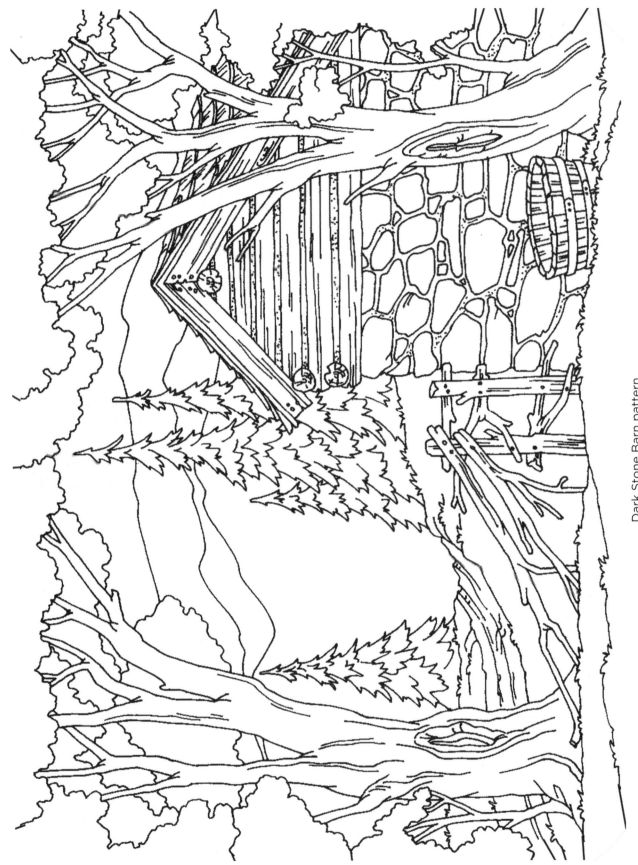

Dark Stone Barn pattern
© LORA S. IRISH

Dark Stone Barn shading guide

© LORA S. IRISH

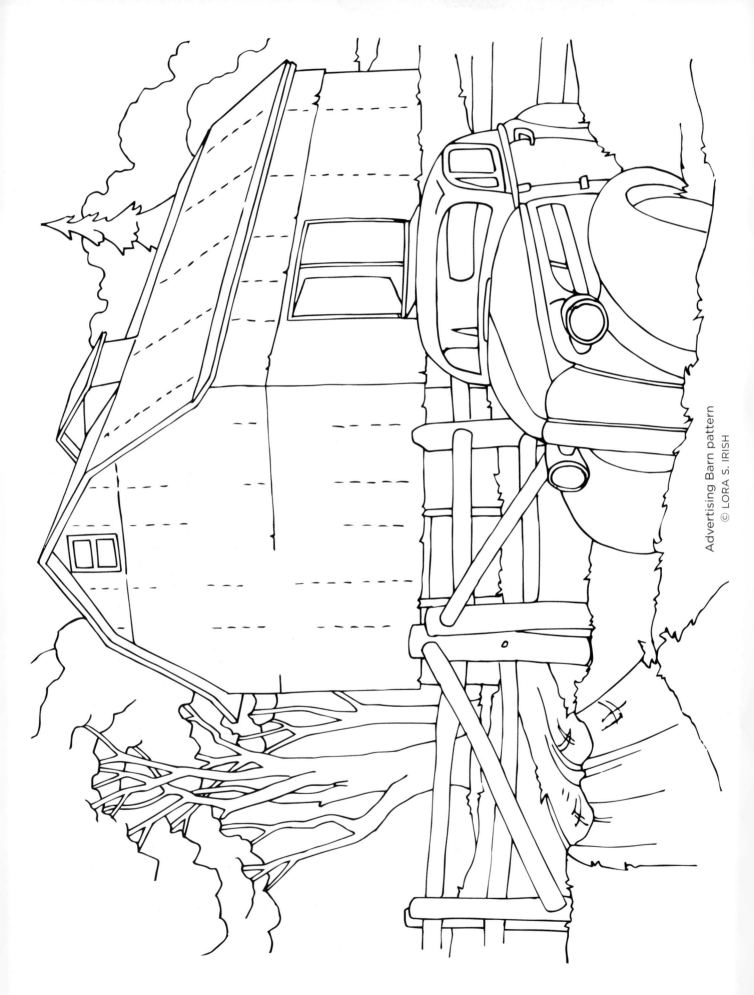

Advertising Barn pattern
© LORA S. IRISH

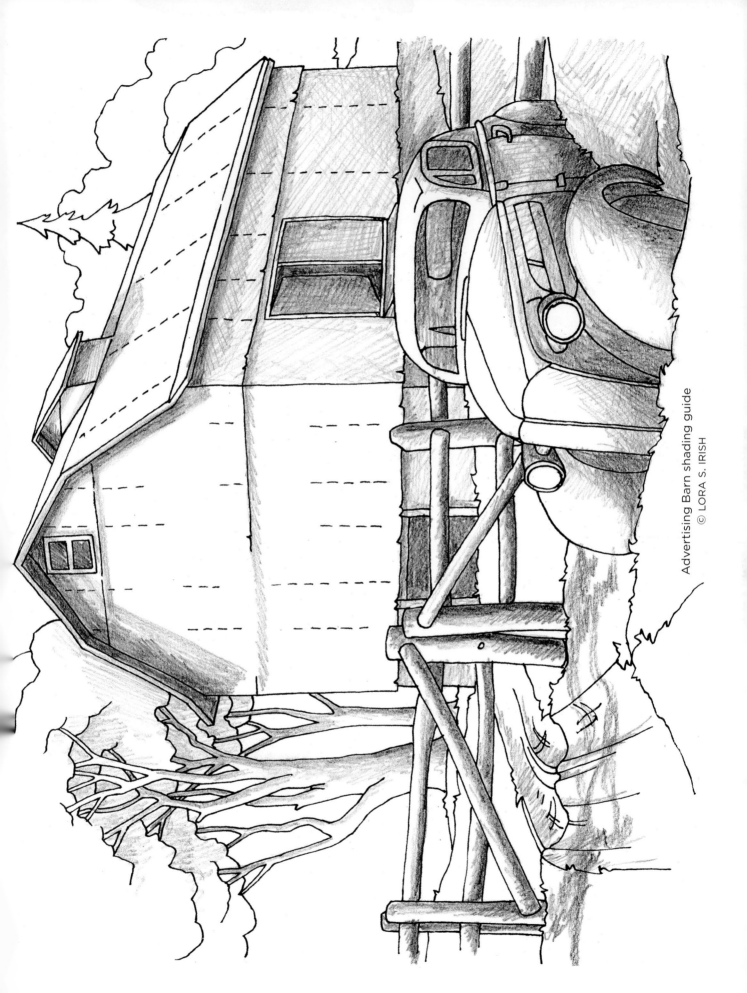

Advertising Barn shading guide
© LORA S. IRISH

Bank Barn pattern
© LORA S. IRISH

Blue Jay Pond pyrography
© LORA S. IRISH

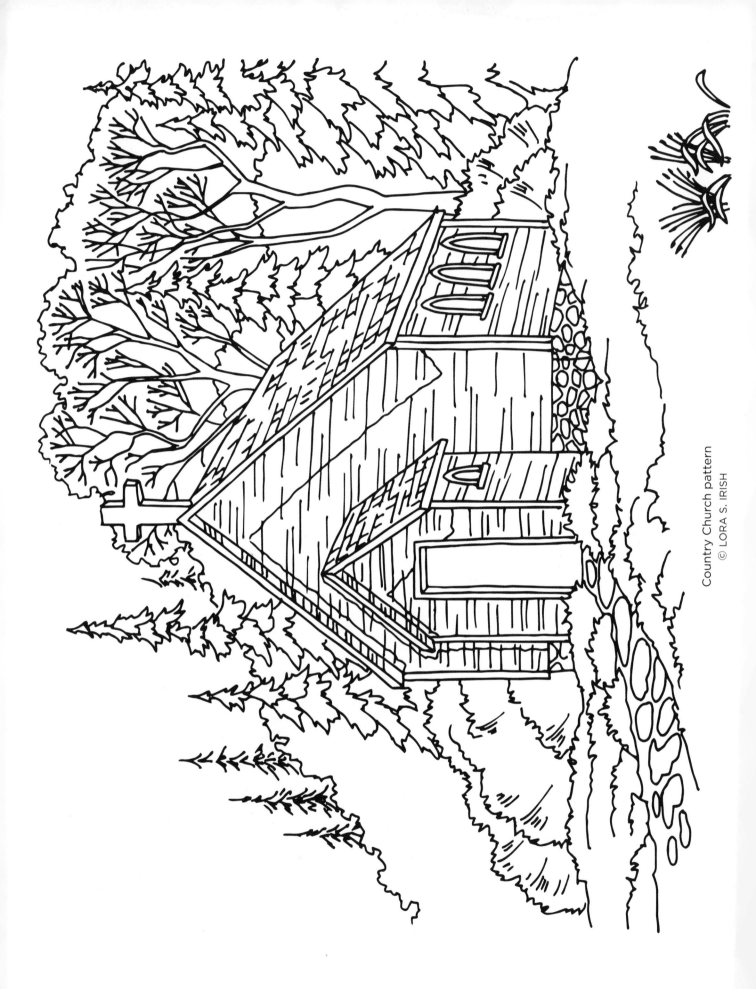

Country Church pattern
© LORA S. IRISH

Country Church pyrography
© LORA S. IRISH

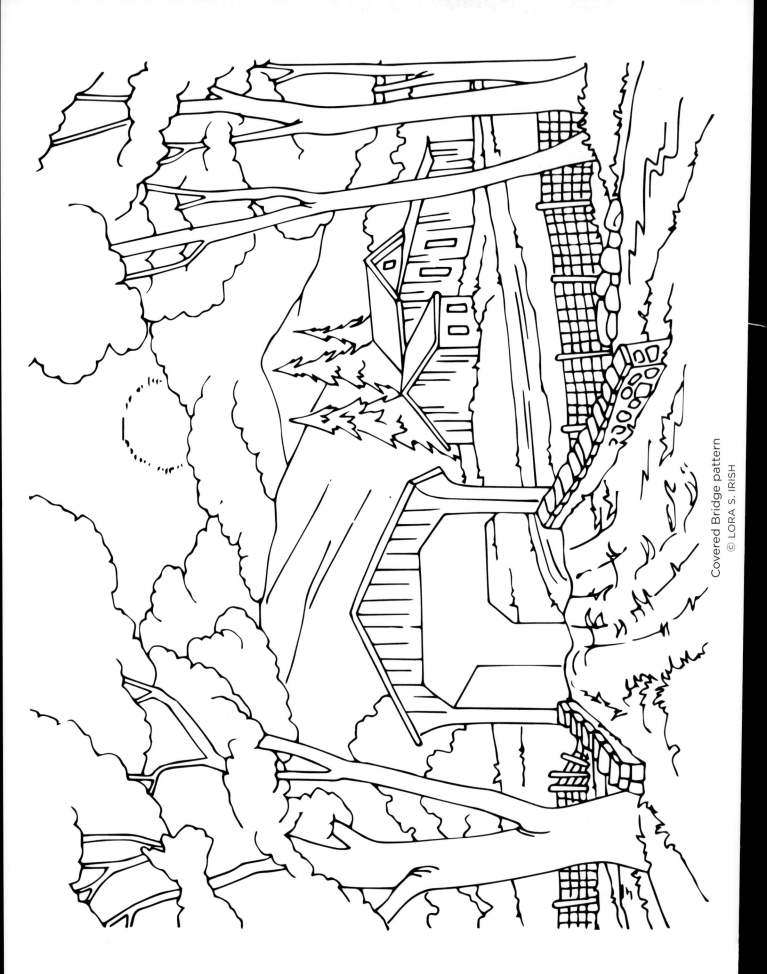

Covered Bridge pattern
© LORA S. IRISH

Covered Bridge pyrography
© LORA S. IRISH

Duck Pond pattern
© LORA S. IRISH

Duck Pond pyrography
© LORA S. IRISH

End of Road pattern

© LORA S. IRISH

End of Road pyrography
© LORA S. IRISH

Grandpa's Pride pattern
© LORA S. IRISH

Grandpa's Pride pyrography
© LORA S. IRISH

Elizabethtown Star Barn pattern
© LORA S. IRISH

Elizabethtown Star Barn pyrography
© LORA S. IRISH

Home Sweet Home pattern
© LORA S. IRISH

Home Sweet Home pyrography
© LORA S. IRISH

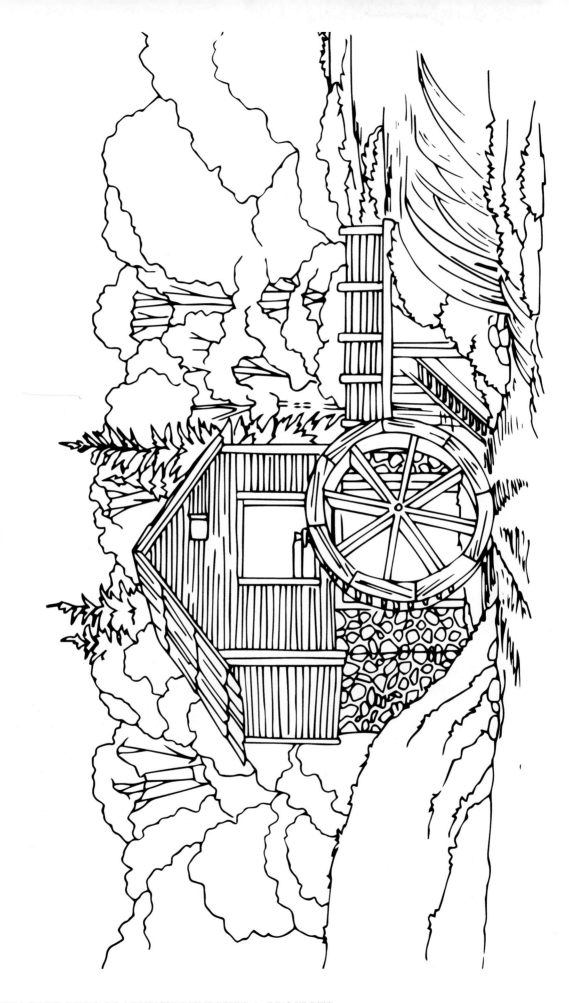

Mill Wheel Pond pattern
© LORA S. IRISH

Mill Wheel Pond pyrography
© LORA S. IRISH

Old Truck pattern
© LORA S. IRISH

Old Truck pyrography

© LORA S. IRISH

Our Town pattern (top)
© LORA S. IRISH

Our Town pyrography (bottom)
© LORA S. IRISH

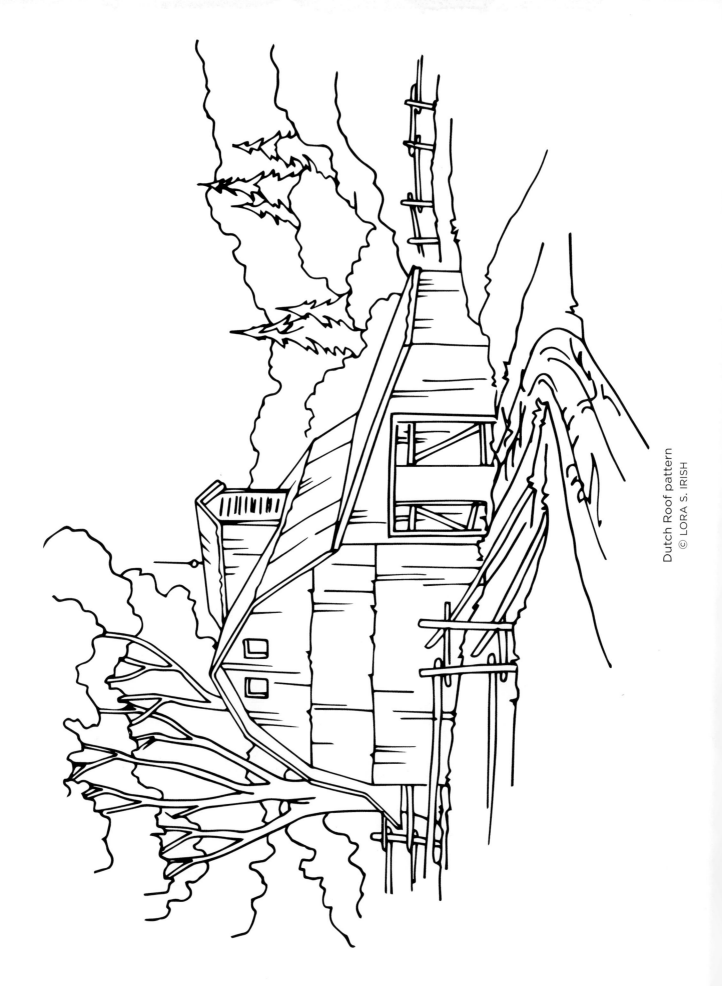

Dutch Roof pattern
© LORA S. IRISH

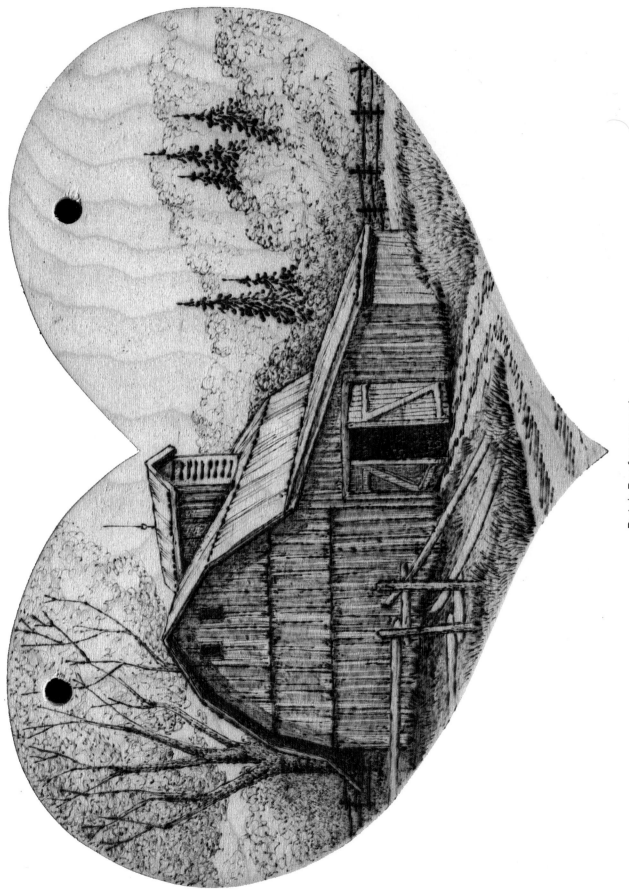

Dutch Roof pyrography
© LORA S. IRISH

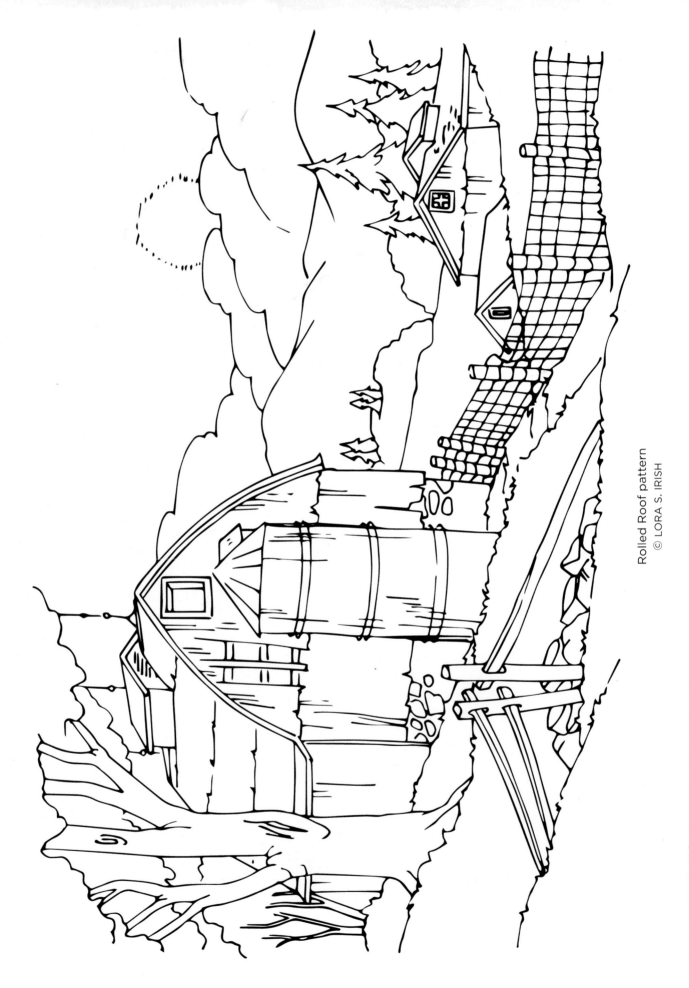

Rolled Roof pattern

© LORA S. IRISH

Blue Jay Pond pattern
© LORA S. IRISH

Bank Barn shading guide
© LORA S. IRISH

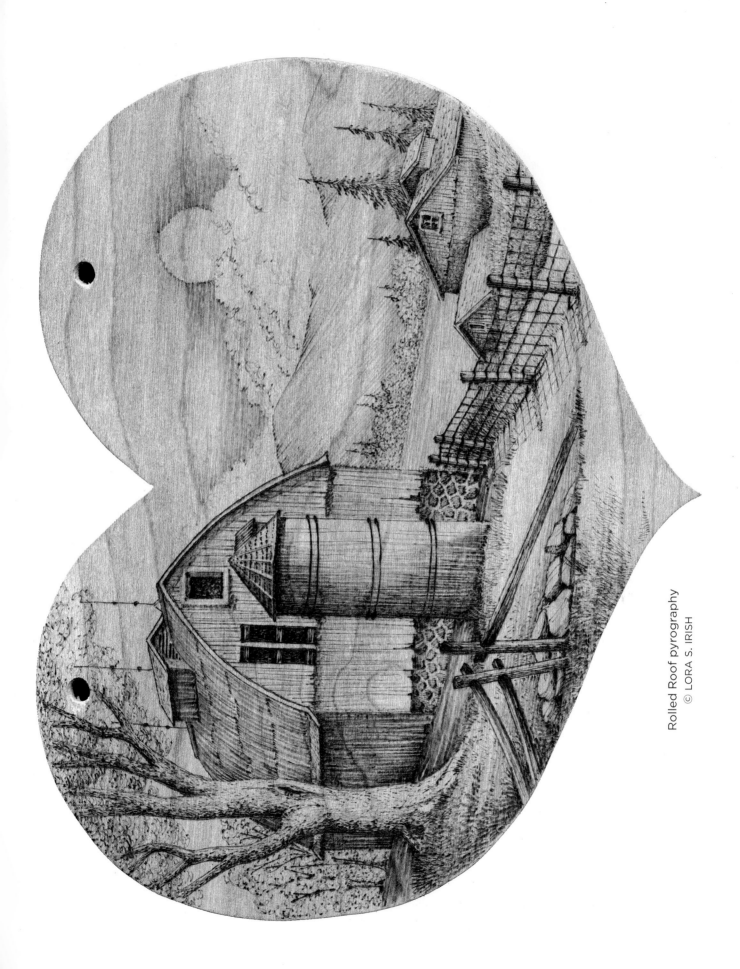

Rolled Roof pyrography
© LORA S. IRISH

Sailboat pattern
© LORA S. IRISH

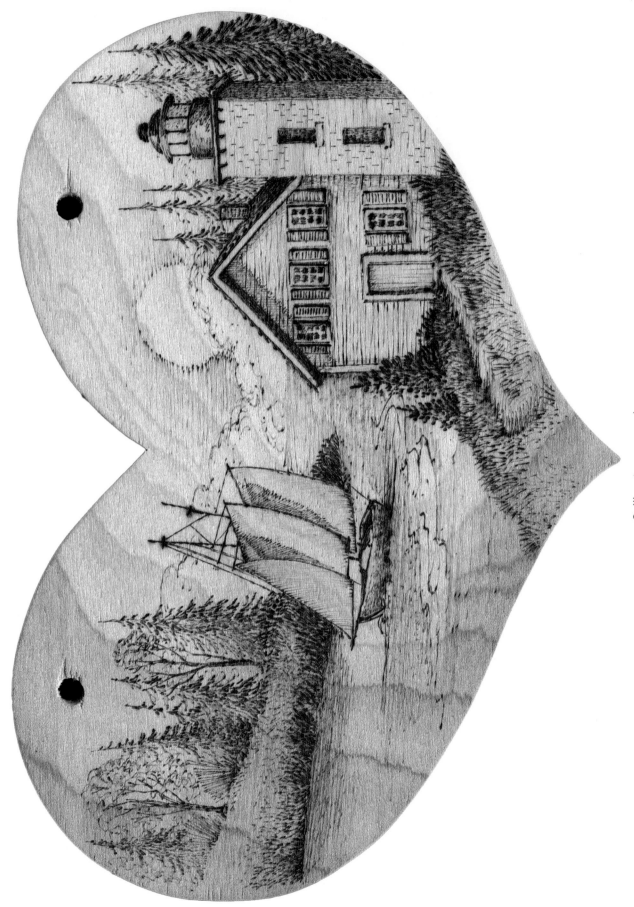

Sailboat pyrography
© LORA S. IRISH

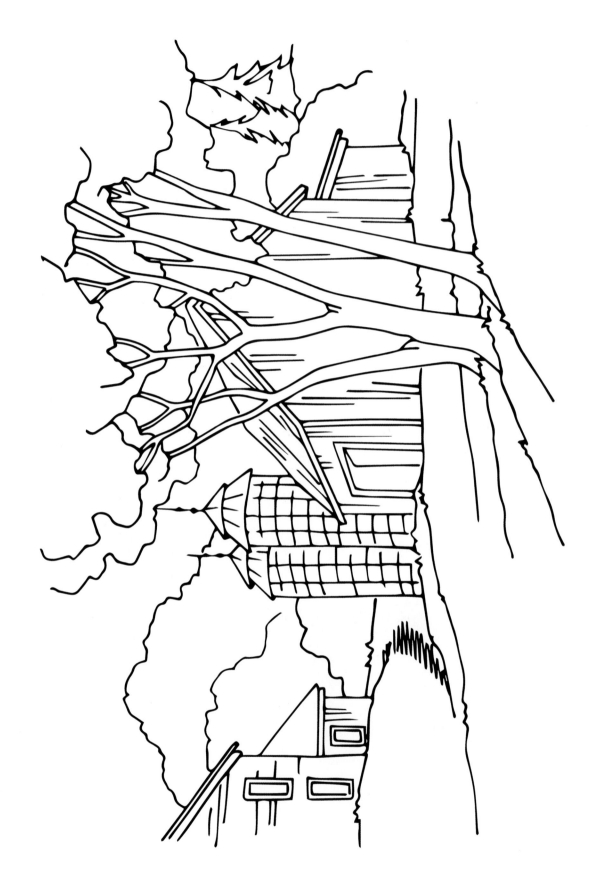

Garage pattern
© LORA S. IRISH

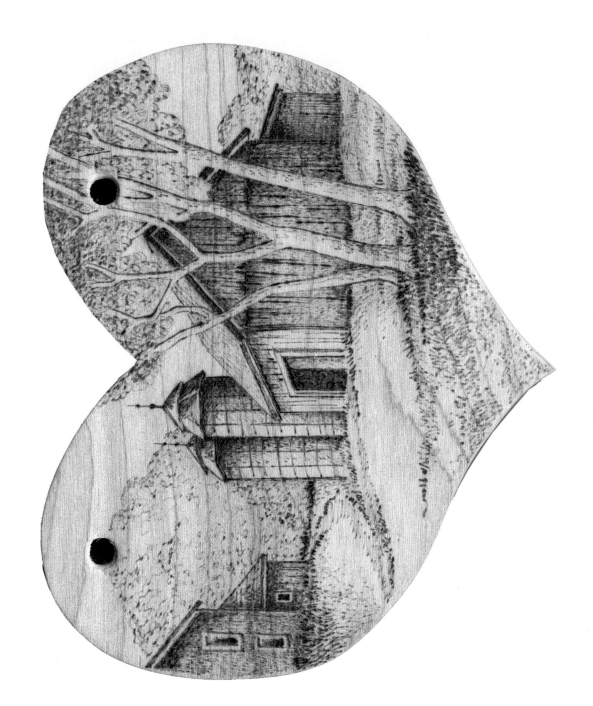

Garage pyrography
© LORA S. IRISH

Outhouse pattern
© LORA S. IRISH

Lighthouse pattern
© LORA S. IRISH

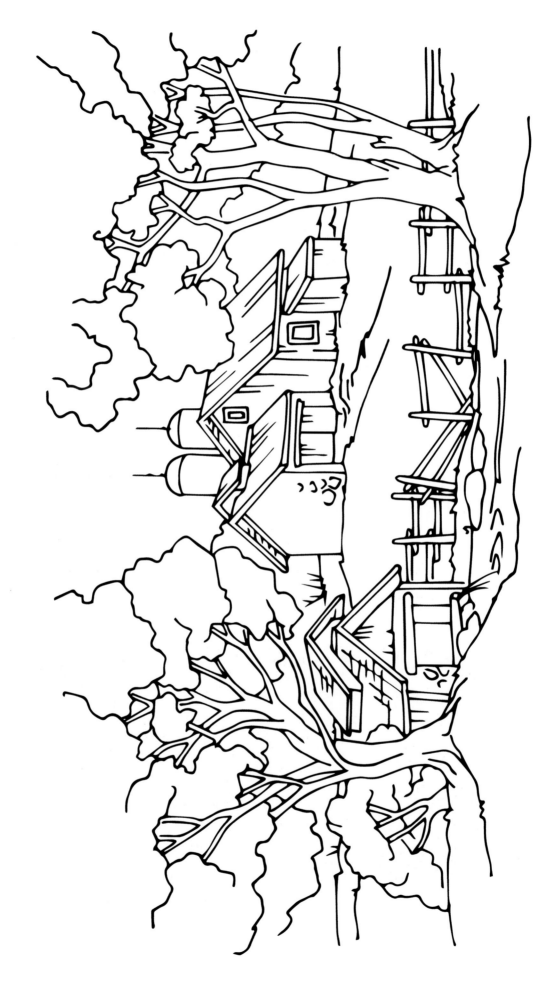

Distant Barn pattern
© LORA S. IRISH

Ramshackle Barn pattern
© LORA S. IRISH

ABOUT THE AUTHOR

Internationally known artist Lora S. Irish is the author of 28 woodcarving, pyrography, and craft pattern books, including *Great Book of Carving Patterns*, *World Wildlife Patterns for the Scroll Saw*, *The Art and Craft of Pyrography*, *Relief Carving the Wood Spirit*, *Great Book of Celtic Patterns*, and many more. Winner of the Woodcarver of the Year award, Lora is a frequent contributor to *Woodcarving Illustrated* and *Scroll Saw Woodworking & Crafts* magazines. Working from her rural mid-Maryland home studio, she is currently exploring new crafts and hobbies, including wire bent link jewelry, metal sheet jewelry, piece patch and appliqué quilting, gourd carving, gourd pyrography, and leather crafts.

Safety Resources

American Association of Poison Control Centers: www.aapcc.org

Poison Help: www.poisonhelp.hrsa.gov

The Wood Database, Toxicity of Wood Species:
www.wood-database.com/wood-articles/wood-allergies-and-toxicity

Toxic Woods, HSE Information Sheet: www.hse.gov.uk/pubns/wis30.pdf

American Woodturner post by Bruce Taylor:
www.cs.rochester.edu/u/roche/rec.wood.misc/wood.toxic

Pallet Wood Toxicity: www.instructables.com/id/How-to-determine-if-a-wood-pallet-is-safe-for-use

Pallet Wood Safety: http://diyready.com/how-to-know-if-a-pallet-is-safe

Common Toxic Chemicals and Finishes, Environmentally Sound Finishes: www.greenhomeguide
.com/know-how/article/selecting-healthy-and-environmentally-sound-finishes

Wood Toxicity and How to Protect Yourself: www.woodworkerssource.com/wood_toxicity.php

Paint, Lacquer, and Varnish Remover Poisoning:
www.nlm.nih.gov/medlineplus/ency/article/002801.htm

Environmentally Safe Oil Varnishes:
www.brighthub.com/environment/green-living/articles/64002.aspx

Toxicity in Craft Gourds: www.arlingtongourdpatch.webs.com/gourdsafety.htm

INDEX

Note: Page numbers in *italics* indicate practice boards, projects, and patterns.